S0-BJL-546

Connecticut River Valley Doorways

Frontispiece [5] Doorway of the Reverend Eliphalet Williams house, East Hartford, Connecticut, ca. 1750. (photograph before 1906)

Connecticut River Valley Doorways
An Eighteenth-Century Flowering

Amelia F. Miller

Published by Boston University
for the Dublin Seminar for New England Folklife.

FERNALD LIBRARY
COLBY-SAWYER COLLEGE
NEW LONDON. N.H. 03257

NA
3020
.M54

This publication was made possible in part through the sale of subscription copies to the following museums, historical societies, and individuals: Historic Deerfield, Inc.; Connecticut Valley Historical Museum; Pocumtuck Valley Memorial Association; Connecticut Historical Society; Wethersfield Historical Society; The Henry Francis du Pont Winterthur Museum; Old Sturbridge Village; Joseph Peter Spang; and Mr. and Mrs. Donald R. Friary.

Copies are available by mail from Boston University Scholarly Publications, 985 Commonwealth Avenue, Boston, Massachusetts 02215. Price $9 each, plus $.75 postage and handling charge per copy.

Copyright © 1983 by The Dublin Seminar for New England Folklife and by the Trustees of Boston University.

ISBN 0-87270-053-4

94200

Contents

Foreword

Very few manifestations of sub-regional material culture on the colonial Atlantic seaboard have appealed to the popular imagination more than the distinctive houses built in the Connecticut River Valley just before the Revolution. As author Amelia Miller makes clear, the boundaries of the "valley culture" are somewhat more extensive than the topographical limitations of the river basin itself. These geographical complexities, however, embracing areas of the Berkshires, for example, are readily explained in terms of family and artisanal ties. In any event, the houses themselves with their monumentally important doorways stand in the sharpest possible contrast to any other sub-regional architectural expressions of the eighteenth century on the East Coast.

Earlier writings, beginning with Fiske Kimball's *Domestic Architecture of the American Colonies and of the Early Republic*, published in 1922, have identified both the Connecticut River Valley style and its representative examples. Mrs. Miller, however, has accepted the greater challenge of a definitive study of the subject in terms of its sources, its spread and development, and above all, the key role played by the builders themselves, a significant number of whom she has identified by name and background. The builders in turn have been evaluated in juxtaposition with their clients who, it has been shown, were part of a tight-knit, inward-looking, hierarchically organized valley society — a microcosmic world of which the artisans were an integral part.

It is impossible to stand before the door from the Daniel Fowler house in Westfield, for example, on exhibit since the 1920s in the American Wing of the Metropolitan Museum of Art in New York, and not be easily moved to make comparison with such stylish monuments as Sparhawk Hall in Kittery, Maine, and the Hancock house in Boston. Yet these two contemporary buildings on the coast and the Westfield doorway are in many respects the products of two differing societies — certainly of differing sets of perceptions.

It is useless to search for cognitive links with the neatly ordered (though somewhat eclectic) neo-Palladian world of gentleman-architect Peter Harrison and the working habits of cosmopolitan master builders of the eighteenth century who turned regularly to such formal English publications as James Gibbs and the popular pattern books of Batty Langley. One of Mrs. Miller's most important contributions has been her careful analytical study of the valley doorways and other decorative detail and her well reasoned arguments as to why we must rule out bookish sources except in a few very special cases.

Her study of this brief period in New England's architectural history, reaching its peak in the 1750s and '60s, will go a long way to furnish important answers to questions about the nature of the vernacular experience in colonial America. The clearly demonstrated nourishment of this eighteenth-century architectural tradition in the valley by the preceding generation of indigenous furniture makers and decorators furnishes a distinctive revelation of the way the vernacular builder — or the provincial builder, if you prefer — approaches the problem at hand. In more purely art historical terms, we realize that these same builders, while preserving not a little feeling for the plasticity and movement of the baroque forms which are their ultimate models, nevertheless conceived the focal decorative elements themselves in a purely two-dimensional patternistic way. It is this unorthodox mixture of traits which makes the Connecticut River Valley doorways unique.

Thomas Salmon, who emigrated from Chippenham, Wilts., to Stratford, Connecticut, emerges as a shadowy yet provocative actor on the stage and raises perhaps more questions than can readily be answered by the documented remains of his work. He may indeed be a fountainhead, responsible for the introduction of the broken scroll doorway, subsequently diffused throughout the valley.

This and other arguments will continue, fueled by a burgeoning interest in English vernacular building which has identified in isolated rural pockets rather startling contemporary equivalents of the Connecticut Valley work. Mrs. Miller acknowledges these current discoveries and has suggested that parallels exist also in the ancient classical world. Over and beyond any lingering questions, however, is the simple, overriding impact of the data itself which Mrs. Miller has set before us. Comprehensive in its scope, her exhaustive study of the builders and the buildings has put us well on the road to a final understanding of a richly creative American phenomenon which has long exercised our curiosity.

Abbott Lowell Cummings
Executive Director
Society for the Preservation
of New England Antiquities

Preface

During the course of this study of eighteenth-century Connecticut River Valley doorways, begun in 1958, each and every town librarian, local historian, every person who responded to letters of inquiry, every helpful museum and historical society curator, and especially every home owner who opened a door to my knock and not only permitted me to photograph and to measure doorways but also invited me to view the house interior, all individuals and organizations that graciously loaned early photographs to be copied, all these persons must know how fondly I remember them and how grateful I remain.

Of those who deserve special recognition, the first is Anthony Junker, architect of Philadelphia and a 1957 Summer Fellow of the Heritage Foundation in Deerfield, Massachusetts, who first called attention to the possibility of a relationship of the triangular pedimented doorway on the John Sheldon house (Sheldon Hawks) in Deerfield with a builder's guide and who may thus be considered to have set doorway research in motion.

For the two summers of 1958 and 1959, another Heritage Foundation Fellow, Donald L. Bunse, presently of Missoula, Montana, helped to pioneer this doorway research as together we groped with myths both local and widespread (some Englishman came over and made all of our doorways in Connecticut — the crossed panels on the doors are Christian crosses — those crosses at the bottom were to ward off witches — Christopher Wren designed this doorway) and as we hesitatingly inquired of architectural historians as to whether such a study had not indeed been accomplished long ago and received negative answers.

Ten years after the search for doorways and their history had begun, the summer of 1968 was spent measuring doorways of the Connecticut River Valley style in the attempt, to equate local measurements and ratios with proportions suggested in various builders' guides. Nathaniel M. Sims and Charles R. Miller climbed the ladder as I recorded from below.

By far and away the two persons who have been most deeply involved with me in research on what someone long ago, in all innocence, called my scroll "impediments" are my friends Abbott Lowell Cummings and William Lamson Warren. Abbott combed the photographic collections of The Society for the Preservation of New England Antiquities, responded to theories, and posed questions that frequently led to late evening discussions as my livingroom took on the look of a jungle with books and files heaped everywhere. Bill greeted me on my Wednesday trips to Hartford with new material from the archives of the Connecticut Historical Society and shared with me helpful friends and acquaintances all over Connecticut.

With Bill perhaps the most triumphant moment of all took place on 13 July 1960 when through combined efforts of detection Bill and I drove to a shed in Glastonbury, Connecticut, and there found, as by then expected, the long stored away scroll doorway from the Reverend Eliphalet Williams house from East Hartford, now installed at the Connecticut Historical Society.

Sentimental memories of research excursions with both Abbott and Bill abound. The support, help, and encouragement of these two friends cannot be measured.

In the last two years Kevin Sweeney has been an immense help in sorting out problems in the Wethersfield, Connecticut, area. Consistently responding promptly to specific questions, Kevin has shared broader ideas as we have discussed our mutual interest — the Connecticut River Valley.

Finally, there is Peter Benes who has rescued my research on Connecticut River Valley doorways from certain demise in files and notebooks. His interest, faith, and patience have all been exceptional. Thank you Peter Benes.

Amelia F. Miller
Deerfield
1982

Introduction

In the mid-eighteenth century a distinct and unmistakable style of doorway developed in the Connecticut River Valley in New England. Although not strictly confined to towns along the Connecticut River, this particular style flourished in its purest form from Wethersfield, Connecticut, north to Deerfield, Massachusetts. As valley joiners migrated into the western parts of Connecticut and Massachusetts and as men who had moved into those western areas commissioned joiners in the valley to build doorways, the style was carried beyond the river. Tangential examples were constructed in Connecticut towns along Long Island Sound; and in certain areas, as around Farmington, Connecticut, regional characteristics developed. But only in towns along the river, well established by the mid-eighteenth century, did the true Connecticut River Valley doorway dominate. Bold and innovative, these doorways were rooted in the classical tradition and seem related in spirit to artisan manneristic gateways and doorways much favored in England in the previous century.[1] They bear little resemblance, however, to doorways of the same period found one hundred miles to the east in coastal Massachusetts and Rhode Island towns.

While the scroll pedimented doorway is regarded as the most typical of the Connecticut River Valley styles, it was only one of several pediment variants. A triangular pediment was actually more common than a scroll pediment and appears to have been a slightly earlier form. On rare occasions a segmental pediment was substituted. As time went on, doorways were constructed with no pediment at all. A large number of so-called flat-top doorways are known to have had a pediment originally, but others that reach to within inches of the window above clearly had none.

It is the scroll pediment, however, that represents the greatest overall accomplishment of the eighteenth-century Connecticut River Valley house joiner. Trained to execute all manner of decorative work for a house or public building (window pediments, stairways, panelling, pilastered chimney breasts, cornices, panelled summer beams, cupboards, and pulpits), at least some house joiners are known to have also made furniture in addition to architectural trim.[2] But the house joiner perhaps summoned his most exacting efforts in designing and building the high, curved scrolls and accompanying decorative work that make these doorways outstanding examples of the joiner's craft.

Of the slightly over two hundred doorways of all varieties known from surviving examples and from sources such as paintings, photographs, drawings, architectural fragments, and literary descriptions, sixty-six had scroll pediments. Of these, only twenty-three survive: ten in museums or historical societies, thirteen on the houses for which they were constructed. Of the thirteen still attached to houses, only eleven may be regarded as basically unaltered.

There is no way to determine how many of these scroll pediments originally existed in the eighteenth century, but surely more than those now known. The town of Hatfield, Massachusetts, home of the joiner Samuel Partridge to whom are attributed doorways both in Hatfield and in other towns, had as many as six surviving on the village street in the late nineteenth century. But Hatfield may not be typical. Certainly there were doorways, now lost, in towns experiencing considerable urban development prior to the age of photography, such as Hartford, Connecticut, and Springfield, Massachusetts. But other forces were also responsible for these losses. Many pediments were undoubtedly destroyed when front porches became fashionable in the nineteenth century, and changing fashion also determined that many houses with doorways were torn down to be replaced by a new residence. Fire, general deterioration, and rot also took their toll. In 1914 boys with firecrackers on the Fourth of July wrecked the then deserted Churchill house (20) in Newington, Connecticut.

The agents that managed to save and preserve the known surviving pedimented doorways have been equally diverse. Sentiment must have prompted late-nineteenth-century residents of the David Judson house (33) in Stratford, Connecticut, to apply the early pediment to the gable of a Victorian porch where it remained until the porch was ultimately removed, at which time the pediment was returned to its rightful position over the front door.

Judging by the number of dwelling houses and public buildings with scroll doorways that were recorded in paintings and drawings during the nineteenth century, these doorways were even then regarded by some as important landmarks of the community. It was not until the early twentieth century, however, that antiquarians and dealers began to recognize their true worth. When in 1916 the Metropolitan Museum of Art purchased from Charles Woolsey Lyon the scroll pedimented doorway removed from the Daniel Fowler house (63) in Westfield, Massachusetts, the Connecticut River Valley doorway was brought to the attention of a wide audience. Subsequently, several scroll doorways were rescued from houses destined to be demolished and were installed in other major museums.

In the Connecticut River Valley the times were right in the middle of the eighteenth century for such outward manifestations of wealth and security as these pedimented doorways. The Indian wars that directly and personally had affected valley settlements were all but over. Men of means and position — ministers, merchants, those in professions, and those of rank in the Colonial Militia — could now afford to employ joiners to decorate their homes with fine panelling, shell-carved cupboards, and elaborate doorways. Accordingly, these same men, frequently appointed to building committees for meeting houses, churches, and other public edifices, were also responsible for selecting pedimented doorways for those structures. And joiners in the valley were quick to take note of and to imitate architectural features in large towns to the east. The scroll pedimented doorway executed in stone for the balcony of Thomas Hancock's house on Beacon Hill in Boston has long been cited, and perhaps overemphasized, as an influence on doorways in the valley.

What Connecticut River Valley joiners did not know was that the practice of decorating doorways with a pediment was ancient, at least as ancient as the monumental Lion Gate at Mycenae of about 1250 B.C. Nor did he know that a scroll-like pediment was painted as an entrance to the world beyond on a wall at Boscoreale near Pompeii about 60 B.C. And if the Connecticut River Valley joiner could have known that a hint of the scroll pediment was constructed in fifteenth-century Italy on the Ducal Palace at Urbino, he probably would have attached little relevance to it. Even had the Connecticut River Valley joiner known that elaborately pedimented gateways and doorways had been designed by Serlio in Italy in the sixteenth century, the significance would have escaped him.

Both the Connecticut River Valley joiner and his patron did know, however, that the scroll pedimented doorway was to be found in England on stately homes such as Uppark in Sussex and closer at hand on houses like Sparhawk Hall in Kittery, Maine. Builders of such houses as Sparhawk Hall designed doorways by using architectural pattern books or builders' guides that were published in England and imported into the colonies. By studying these books it was possible for the joiner on the east coast to render a faithful copy of a printed plate. A comparison of a design given in William Salmon's *Palladio Londinensis* with the doorway on Sparhawk Hall reveals striking similarities in the general proportions, the pilasters, and the abbreviated scrolls in each pediment.

When, on the other hand, the doorway on Sparhawk Hall is compared to a typical scroll pedimented doorway of the Connecticut River Valley — that on the Elijah Williams house (48) in Deerfield — the characteristics of the valley doorway become apparent. Noticeable are the pilasters with high panelled pedestals and fluting separated by a heavy ogee molding, a decorated pilaster cap, a decorated keystone, several bands of fascia in the architrave, a pulvinated frieze, a decorated cornice, a rusticated surround, double-leaf doors, and in this case a scroll pediment with an ornamental finial and rosettes at the termination of the scrolls. Expense and preference determined whether the entire doorway was to be doubled, a decorative device to give the illusion of depth or to set the doorway in relief. For doorways of the Connecticut River Valley style there was no rule, but each doorway shares a majority, if not all, of the above features.

One may well ask why the Connecticut River Valley joiner failed to copy so faithfully from his builder's guide as did his counterpart on the east coast. The answer is clearly not because the valley joiner lacked a basic skill with his working tools or, more important, the mathematical knowledge to execute doorways as illustrated in architectural pattern books. To modify successfully was more difficult than to copy.

Three mathematical calculations were involved in the construction of a scroll pediment: the height of the basic triangle from which each scroll is formed, the point of inflection or point at which the curve reverses, and the distance between the two basic triangles. Consider-

Figure 1 Design for a doorway. From William Salmon, *Palladio Londinensis*, seventh edition, 1767. Plate XXVI. (The first edition was issued in London, 1734.)

Figure 2 Doorway from the Nathaniel Sparhawk house (Sparhawk Hall), Kittery, Maine, built ca. 1742. (photograph 1930s)

ing that an alteration by so much as a few inches of any one of these factors could throw the whole off balance, the pleasingly proportioned results achieved by the Connecticut River Valley joiner leave little doubt as to his ability with his compass, an ability perhaps greater than that of those who followed builders' guides more literally.

Fundamental modifications were not made arbitrarily. The Connecticut River Valley joiner was obliged to adapt doorway proportions to accommodate double-leaf doors. An ancient form, traces of double doors have been found in Bronze Age palaces on Crete and on a threshold at Akrotiri, the village on the island of Thera buried by volcanic eruption about 1500 B.C. Double-leaf doors were in continuous use, largely on religious buildings, from the time of Imperial Rome down through the Middle Ages and Renaissance. In England builders through the centuries employed double-leaf doors, including Wren in the seventeenth century, but double doors were not commonly illustrated in builders' guides in the eighteenth century.

Double-leaf doors occasionally made an appearance on the east coast, whereas in the Connecticut River Valley the use of double doors at the main entrance had become widespread by the mid-eighteenth century.[3] The advantage of double doors opening into the narrow front entry of a center-chimney house is obvious, but in the Connecticut River Valley double doors were used on houses with center halls as well. The reason for this preference in the valley when the need no longer existed is not entirely clear. Perhaps the explanation is simply that residents in the valley, having become accustomed to double doors, merely clung to the familiar form. But it may be that as wide double doors emphasized the importance of meeting houses and other imposing public buildings, their presence on a dwelling was considered an enhancement to the architectural stature of the house as it also indirectly proclaimed the owner's elevated position in a given community. Whatever the reason for double doors in the Connecticut River Valley, the resulting widened door opening forced the valley joiner to deviate from published ratios and to make his own adjustments.

An entirely different factor, unrelated to proportion, was responsible for the individuality of decorative detail on Connecticut River Valley doorways. Although joiners clearly had a full grasp of mathematical principles, their geographical situation in the valley, so far removed from European intellectual sources, prevented any thorough understanding or reverence for the sanctity of classical rules. From builders' guides a classical vocabulary was available, a concept of the orders; but Vitruvius, Alberti, Serlio, Palladio, Inigo Jones, and even the later Englishmen who published architectural guides, Batty Langley, Edward Hoppus, and William Salmon among others, were helpful experts only, not law-makers.

Without realizing he was committing a form of architectural heresy, the valley joiner solved his particular problems as he freely translated published decorative formulas without compunction. He probably attempted to imitate a Corinthian capital when he carved foliage pilaster caps like those on the Samuel (Eleazer) Porter house (50) in Hadley, Massachusetts. He was almost certainly inspired by a plate in Batty Langley's *Gothic Architecture*, published in London in 1742, when he executed vine-carved pilasters like those on the Elihu White house (56) in Hatfield; but he was also aware of a vernacular vine-like carving on joined furniture still much in evidence of a generation or two earlier, now known as Hadley chests.

Bearing in mind then all of these intermingling forces — the three variable mathematical principles that determine the appearance of a scroll pediment, the need to adapt builders' guide proportions to accommodate double-leaf doors, classical rules only partially comprehended, the influence of traditional design patterns of previous generations — it is apparent that the individual Connecticut River Valley joiner was given a wide latitude as he planned a doorway. It follows logically to ask why, then, there should be so striking a similarity of proportion and decorative detail up and down the valley. If these Connecticut River Valley doorways differ so prominently from published patterns and from doorways to the east, why do they differ so little amongst themselves? Or, in other words, why is there a Connecticut River Valley style? Why should the proportion and detail of a doorway such as on the Simeon Belden house (41) in Wethersfield, resemble so closely that on the Elijah Williams house (48) in Deerfield? What can account for similar details not illustrated in builders' guides that appear in widely separated areas?

It certainly is not by chance that the keystone on the Simeon Belden house doorway (41) and that on the doorway of the David Sexton house (186) in Deerfield are so similar and are only two of a considerable number taking the same form. Similarities in the valley are far too striking to be coincidental. The foliage decorated pilaster cap on the Samuel Porter house (50) in Hadley is reproduced in Stockbridge to the west in the Berkshires on the Reverend John Sergeant house (61). Doors with notched or jagged "S" panels on the Ebenezer Grant house (29) in South Windsor, Connecticut, match those on the Daniel Fowler doorway (63) from Westfield. An even more surprising detail is shared by these last two doorways: instead of a panel, each pedestal contains a miniature scroll doorway.

Elsewhere, a fan at the base of the fluting on pilasters that appears on the Luke Thrall house (137) in East Granby, Connecticut, is also present miles to the east on the Reverend John Willard house (168) in Stafford, Connecticut, and is found far to the north on the Richard

Church house (197) in Hatfield, as well. Triangular pediments on doorways and on windows were occasionally decorated with a slim vertical
piece reaching from the center of the base to the apex where in the soffit of the triangle a projection of the bed molding spreads outward to
resemble the outline of an elm tree. This device is found in the
Massachusetts towns of Longmeadow, Springfield, and Northampton
and in Suffield, Connecticut.

Not only in decorative detail but also in overall proportion the doorways on the Elijah Williams house (48) in Deerfield and the Simeon
Wait house (55) in Hatfield appear nearly identical. The scroll
pediments have the same mushroom-shaped finial set on a panelled
base and the same six-petal rosettes at the termination of the scrolls.
The rusticated surrounds are identical as are the three-channelled
keystones and panelled pedestals. Moldings in each entablature are
similar and the six-petal rosettes in the pilaster caps have the same
centers. Measurements confirm the visual impression.[4]

The answer to the question of homogeneity of doorways in the Connecticut River Valley suggests itself. Doorway joiners travelled from
town to town, not as did the wandering nineteenth-century painter in
search of work and bed and board, but at the request of men who wish-
ed to employ their special talents, and doorway joiners also migrated
westward. That these joiners were sent for further suggests that a
limited number of house joiners made a practice of constructing doorways.

A pattern slowly emerges that can be sparsely but adequately
documented. Samuel Partridge, for instance, was born in Hadley and
probably trained as a joiner in Wethersfield. In the fall of 1754 Partridge accompanied two joiners from Connecticut, Oliver Eason and
Parmenas King, who went to Deerfield and worked for a month on the
house of Elijah Williams. Earlier that year both Eason and King had
worked along with John Steel, Jr., a Longmeadow joiner, on the house
of Samuel Colton of Longmeadow, Massachusetts (57). In 1755 John
Steel, Jr., worked for Josiah Dwight in Springfield, Massachusetts.
When work for Elijah Williams in Deerfield was completed on 5
December 1754, Eason returned to East Hartford. King resumed work
for Samuel Colton in Longmeadow, and Partridge settled in Hatfield
across the river from his native Hadley.

The migration of the joiner Alexander Grant from South Windsor,
Connecticut, to Westfield, Massachusetts, is thought to account for
similar miniature scroll doorways in the pedestals on the Ebenezer
Grant house (29) in South Windsor and on the Daniel Fowler house
(63) in Westfield.

As joiners travelled, worked together, and moved apart again, as
they changed their place of residence, as settlers and joiners alike mov-

ed westward, thus ideas were carried up and down the Connecticut River and beyond. These exchanges are thought to account for the continuity of style of the Connecticut River Valley doorway.

Bounded approximately in time by the doorway on Christ Church (31) in Stratford of about 1744-1749, and by the doorway designed for the 1795 Roxbury, Connecticut, meeting house (26), the scroll pedimented doorway seems to have been favored as an entrance for dwelling houses only during the decades of the 1750s and 1760s. By the turn of the century, scroll doorways, triangular pedimented and even flat-top doorways of the eighteenth-century style had all but ceased to be made. By 1800, with rare exceptions, doorways with all the characteristic trimmings of multi-petal rosettes, foliage carving, rustication, and heavy pulvinated friezes had disappeared as the architectural form known as Connecticut River Valley doorways.

1. See John Summerson, *Architecture in Britain, 1530-1830* (Baltimore, 1954), chap. 10, "Artisan Mannerism, 1615-1675," pp. 97-105.
2. See sections on Oliver Eason, Aaron Grant, Samuel Partridge, and Judah Woodruff in Appendix II of this volume; see also Robert F. Trent, *Hearts and Crowns: Folk Chairs of the Connecticut Coast* (New Haven, 1977), pp. 39-44, for a possible association of Thomas Salmon with furniture making in the area of Stratford, Connecticut.
3. Abbott L. Cummings cites the following houses in eastern Massachusetts: the Boardman house, Saugus (ca. 1687), the White-Ellery house, Gloucester (ca. 1710) where the width of the front entrance indicated former double doors, and the Parson Barnard house, North Andover (ca. 1715), where evidence of pintles was uncovered on both door jambs.
4. During the summer of 1968, measurements were taken from fourteen scroll doorways, fourteen triangular pedimented doorways, including side entrances as well as front, and thirty-four flat-top doorways, some of which formerly had a pediment. Triangular window pediments were also measured. The purpose was to compare proportions of Connecticut River Valley doorways with those suggested in various builders' guides. Not surprisingly, because of the widened entrance occasioned by double-leaf doors, no doorway was found to comply with an English design. In general, however, doorways in the Connecticut River Valley shared strikingly similar proportions among themselves. While no two scroll pedimented doorways measured exactly the same, ratios were consistent. In the case of the scroll pediment, the point of inflection was commonly at about mid-point. The doorways on the Elijah Williams house and the Simeon Wait house are nearly identical in proportion as well as in decorative detail, the latter being merely a slightly scaled-down version of the former; the joiner perhaps took into consideration the slightly smaller facade of the Wait house. The height of triangular pediments was found almost without exception to be one-fourth of the base.

Checklist of Doorways

GUIDELINES

History of House and Doorway.

All known doorways now or formerly standing at the front or main entrance to a dwelling house or public building that meet some if not all of the qualifications named in the Introduction are included in the Checklist regardless of geographical boundaries. Structures are separated according to doorway type and then listed alphabetically by state, by town, and by home owner. Unknown locations and unknown houses appear at the end of each appropriate category. Side or rear doorways of interest and also window pediments are noted under the main doorway listing. When possible, a house is listed by the name of the original owner-builder whose dates, when known, follow his name. Other more familiar names for a house are also included.

While the addition of nineteenth-century front porches suggests that numerous present flat-top doorways probably once had pediments, scroll pediments in particular, some flat-tops having features related to surviving scroll pedimented doorways leave little doubt as to the former pediment. Among these are the doorways on the Noah Smith house in Hadley, Massachusetts, and on the Gen. John Ashley house in Sheffield, Massachusetts. However, unless architectural fragments survive or unless evidence appears on the house (as in the case of the Capt. Thomas Dickinson house, Deerfield, Massachusetts), present flat-top doorways are listed in that category to avoid the possibility of an incorrect attribution, and the suspected pediment is noted. The occasional practice of constructing houses with front and side overhangs lasted well into the eighteenth century; in fact there occurred an overhang "revival" in Farmington, Connecticut, in the 1780s. Throughout the Checklist where doorways are cited as adapted to an overhang, that overhang may be understood to be hewn rather than framed.

Documented dates for houses and doorways are given when known and probable dates are suggested as indicated by style, by a marriage, or by new ownership occasioned by the death of a widow. Suspiciously early dates supplied by nineteenth-century publications or local tradition are questioned in some cases. However, to date a house accurately is not necessarily to date the doorway. The importance of recognizing the years shortly following the death of a widow as a period of possible new construction should be noted. Only upon the death of the widow, who had by law her widow's thirds or rights in a house, might the legal heir perhaps feel free for the first time to make improvements on his property as he finally became the sole owner. For instances of this situation, see descriptions of the Elijah Williams house, Deerfield; the Samuel Porter house, Hadley; the Josiah Dwight house, Springfield — all in Massachusetts and all with scroll pedimented doorways.

For commonly available biographical information, as found in relevant town histories or genealogies, no documentation is included, neither are specific citations for land and probate records where dates and names provided are considered sufficient. Likewise account book references, easily retrievable, are omitted. The sources of all obscure information are supplied. State names are not repeated when they appear in a logical context. The files of Amelia F. Miller are destined for deposit in the library of the Pocumtuck Valley Memorial Association, Deerfield, Massachusetts.

Features.

For doorways still surviving or known from a clear photograph, all features are given with the exception of high panelled pedestals, heavy moldings above pedestals, fluting on pilasters, and a pulvinated frieze, all of which may be assumed; and only deviations are noted. When a doorway is peripheral within the catalogue of characteristics determining the Connecticut River Valley style, this fact is noted and all features are given. For doorways known only from indistinct photographs, drawings, or paintings, all discernible features are listed. If no features are given, it may be understood that none can be distinguished with the exception of the pediment itself. Data concerning replacements, alterations, and other restoration of surviving doorways are drawn from early photographs.

Key to Symbols.

   * indicates doorway survives.
 ** indicates doorway survives on its original house.
  † indicates that the title has been searched.
   Figures in parenthesis refer to checklist entry numbers.

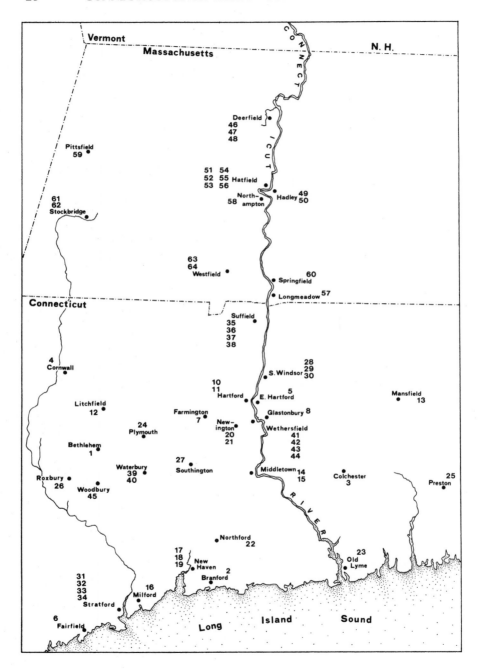

Figure 3   Distribution of scroll pedimented doorways in the Connecticut River Valley.
(Numerals refer to checklist entry numbers.)

Scroll Pedimented Doorways

Connecticut

1. Bethlehem: Second Meeting House.

This meeting house was raised in 1767 and was torn down in 1836. In 1793 the town voted to build a steeple (*Woodbury History*, pp. 248, 257). Early Barber drawings (CHS) show scroll pediments on both the main entrance and on the steeple door.

2. Branford: House of Joseph Frisbie. †

Early photographs labelled Joseph Frisbie house, Branford (one at CHS, one given to AFM by Delphina Clark of Suffield that was taken prior to 1890 by her uncle), show a gambrel-roofed house with a scroll doorway. A Whitefield sketch of the same house (SPNEA) notes, "Supposed to have been built by _____ Harrison about 1775" and "owned by Albinger." The house shown was closely flanked by a house on each side while land records indicate that the only house owned by a Joseph Frisbie in Branford in the eighteenth century stood on a sixty-acre farm and not in an urban area. (The section of Branford where the farm was located is still relatively undeveloped.) The only land purchased by a person named Albinger in Branford was a quarter acre on Maple Street bought by John J. Albinger in 1868 with but a shop on it. The process of title searching is complicated by the absence of Mr. Harrison's first name. Local residents cannot identify the house that is no longer standing in Branford.

Features: (from photographs) double doors.   *Illustrated*

3. Colchester: House of Jonathan Kilbourn (1707-1785). * †

Lurelle V.A. Guild purchased this doorway about 1939 from Charles Kramer of Stamford, Connecticut, and installed it at Milestone Village, Darien. Old photographs (privately owned, copies AFM) show the doorway on a house labelled "Walter J.F. Strong place," give a date of about 1780, and note that the house once belonged to a _____ Goddard. Land and probate records indicated that Walter J.F. Strong purchased the house in 1856, that he mortgaged it to George C. Goddard in 1865, that in 1785 Jonathan Kilbourn left this property to his two sons, Jonathan and David, and that in 1790 Jonathan sold his half of their father's house to David Kilbourn, "it being the house where David now dwells."

The house stood south of Colchester at the top of Strong's Hill on the Param Road until about 1960 when it was torn down.

Features: Ionic volutes in pilaster caps, tapered keystone, multi-petal rosettes at the termination of scrolls, vase-shaped finial, doubled outline, double doors with X panels.

[2]   Joseph Frisbie house, Branford, Connecticut. (photograph ca. 1890)

4.   Cornwall: House of Woodruff Emmons (ca. 1719-1793).

Opposite the meeting house stood a house built in 1758 according to a stone on the front of the chimney bearing that date. Descriptions of the house clearly indicate that the house had a scroll pedimented doorway. "Large massive scrolls and roses of carved work ornamented the tops and sides of the doorways, while the windows, of six by eight glass were surmounted by heavy angular projecting caps. . . ." The house was used as a tavern for many years, but the date when it was torn down is not known; neither is there known to be a photograph of the house. The property was earlier owned by Capt. George Holloway who died in 1756 and who may have begun construction on the house (*Cornwall Records*, p. 247).

Darien: Milestone Village, see Colchester: House of Jonathan Kilbourn (3).

5. East Hartford: House of the Reverend Eliphalet Williams (1727-1803).*†

Land records indicate that the Reverend Eliphalet Williams built a house after 13 February 1750 when he purchased unimproved land and before 19 June 1751 when a deed to adjoining land referred to the first parcel as land "where he [Williams] hath Set up A house for dwelling. . . ." The doorway may have been constructed during this period or within the next few years. In 1906 the house was taken down, but the doorway was purchased by Percy H. Williams, a descendant, who stored it in a shed where it remained until 1960 when Mr. Williams acknowledged the location to William L. Warren and AFM. On 13 July 1960 it was taken to CHS and was later installed there. The house had a gambrel roof, a triangular pediment on the side door, and triangular window pediments with raised corners. *Illustrated*

Features: (from photographs while on house, CHS) pedestals missing, six-petal rosettes in pilaster caps, keystone missing, six-petal rosettes at termination of scrolls, mushroom finial on rectangular pedestal (both now missing), doubled outline, rusticated surround, double doors with X panels (now missing).

[5] The Reverend Eliphalet Williams house, East Hartford, Connecticut, ca. 1750. (photograph before demolition of the house in 1906)

6. Fairfield: House of Elisha T. Mills?

An overmantle from this house shows an unidentified gambrel-roofed house with a scroll doorway (Little, p. 60). Elisha Mills (1733-1816) lived in Huntington, now Shelton, and may have built the house. His son Elisha T. Mills was born in 1764.

7. Farmington: House of Capt. Judah Woodruff (1722-1799).**

Judah Woodruff, joiner and master builder, designer of the 1771 Farmington meeting house, built this house for himself (*Historical Discourse* in Kelly, *Meetinghouses*, 1:162). A marker on the house gives the date 1762. Although the scrolls are not like any others known (the curves including the rosettes are entirely enclosed or outlined by a simple molding), they appear on a photograph of 1906 (*Farmington Homes*); and if they are restorations or additions, the work was done before that year.

Features: Ionic volutes in pilaster caps, duck-bill keystone, rosettes of concentric circles at termination of scrolls, flame finial on rectangular panelled pedestal, double doors with X panels.

8. Glastonbury: House of Gideon Hale (1736-1812).

A photograph (CHS) of a drawing dated 1823 shows a scroll doorway on a house identified only as the Gideon Hale house, Glastonbury.

Features: (from drawing) fluted pilasters, mushroom finial.

9. Greenwich: Meeting House or Church.

A scroll pediment appears on a nineteenth-century painting (privately owned) of a Greenwich meeting house or church, as reported by William L. Warren.

10. Hartford: House of Daniel Bull (ca. 1709-1776).

A nineteenth-century painting of this house and a photograph of a now missing daguerreotype (both CHS) document the existence of this scroll doorway. Information on the reverse of the latter indicates that the house stood on Trinity Street "facing nearly the west end of Elm Street" and that the house was torn down about 1869. In 1786 the house became the property of Isaac Bliss by whose name it was also known (*Colonial Homes*, p. 321). The house is shown on the painting and daguerreotype to have had a triangular pediment on the side door and triangular window pediments.

Hartford: CHS, see East Hartford: House of the Reverend Eliphalet Williams (5).

11. Hartford: House of Thomas Seymour (1705-1767).*

This house, which stood on the west side of Main Street at the south corner of Main and Linden Place, later 123 Main Street, was built by Thomas Seymour about 1750 (see *Hartford History*, pp. 267-68; *Hartford County*, 1:464; *Seymour Family*, p. 81; photograph CHS, Samuel Taylor Collection, Russ house reverse). When the house was demolished (after 1939 when *Seymour Family* was published), the doorway, according to H.A. Armstrong, was purchased by a dealer, Mr. Preston, of Farmington. Later it was bought by Armstrong who sold it to Lloyd Hyde. Mr. Hyde placed it on his house in Old Lyme. Early photographs of the house (CHS) call it the Russ house after a late owner.

Features: six-petal rosettes in pilaster caps, duck-bill keystone, six-petal rosettes at termination of scrolls, spherical finial (similar to mushroom) on rectangular pedestal, doubled outline, single door.

Hartford: WA, see Newington: House of Capt. Charles Churchill (20).

12. Litchfield: Second Meeting House.

This meeting house was probably completed in 1762 and was taken down in 1837 (Kelly, *Meetinghouses*, 1:277). In her autobiography Harriet Beecher Stowe described this meeting house and referred to "its doors with great wooden quirls over them. . . ." Fragments of the pulpit survive (LHS), one a six-petal rosette of the type found from Wethersfield north to Hatfield and Deerfield in Massachusetts may have been the work of James Eason. The scroll doorway may also have been his work.

Illustrated

[12]   Carved pilaster capital from the pulpit of the second meeting house, Litchfield, Connecticut, completed 1762.

13. Mansfield: Meeting House.

A meeting house built in Mansfield 1751-1753 and burned in 1866 (*Mansfield History*) was probably the building pictured by Barber with a scroll doorway and described as the Presbyterian Church (Barber, *Connecticut*, p. 551). There were also triangular window pediments.

14. Middletown: House of Jacob Cornwell (1682-1767). †

A photograph of about 1870, identified as the Jacob Cornwell House (RL), showing ladies in hoop skirts entering a store at the gable end of a house also shows part of a scroll pediment on the front and a triangular pediment over the gable window. A title search indicated that Jacob Cornwell (1735-1808) inherited a house from his father in 1767 and sold it to Jacob Sebor in 1768. This house may have been pulled down by Sebor and a new one built. In 1869 Philip Hoffert leased the house shown in the photograph and operated a store. The house stood at 444 Main Street in 1936 when records of early Middletown houses were compiled (RL), but has since been torn down.

15. Middletown: House of the Reverend Ichabod Camp (1725-1786). †

A Whitefield sketch (SPNEA) showing a gambrel-roofed house with a scroll pediment in Middletown is labelled "The William Plum House. He bought it in 1792 . . . on Main Street near Union Park." Whitefield noted that the house was painted buff, had very large windows, and was very dilapidated. A title search indicated that William Plum, Esq. (1748-1843), purchased the house in 1791 from Mary Leavitt, that in 1753 the Reverend Ichabod Camp purchased the property "Together with a Dwelling House frame partly Covered," and that he sold it in 1760. Richard Alsop owned it from 1760 to 1761, and sold it to Richard Nichols for £ 250. When Nichols sold it in 1767 to Elisha Clark, the price was £ 450, which implies that Nichols improved the house considerably and may have added the doorway.

16. Milford: House of Ephraim Strong (1714-1802).

A house with a scroll pedimented doorway, a side door with a triangular pediment, center chimney, gambrel roof, and three front dormers was illustrated in the *Connecticut Magazine* (November 1899, p. 533). It was entitled the Ephraim Strong House. The date of construction is unknown.

17. New Haven: First Episcopal Church (Trinity Church).

This church was built in 1753 and stood at the east side of Church Street, south of Chapel Street. It was removed in 1817 (Barber, *New Haven*, p. 28). An illustration made prior to 1898 (*New Haven Green*, facing p. 116) shows an elaborate pediment on the main or steeple entrance, and also indicates some form of pediment on a side steeple door.

Features: (from illustration) double doors arched at top.

18. New Haven: State House.

Built of brick in 1763 (Barber, *New Haven*, p. 36), the State House stood front-ing on Temple Street. A circa 1830 painting by William Giles Munson (NHCHS) illustrates the New Haven Green about 1800 and shows a scroll door-way on the main entrance. In 1828 the State House was taken down (*New Haven Green*, p. 153). *Illustrated*

19. New Haven: Third Meeting House.

This brick meeting house was built fronting on Temple Street in 1757 and was removed in 1813 (Barber, *New Haven*, p. 24). An illustration made prior to 1898 (*New Haven Green*, facing p. 96) shows a scroll doorway on the main en-trance in the middle of seven bays. *Illustrated*

[18 and 19]   New Haven Green, New Haven, Connecticut, ca. 1800, showing evidence of scroll pedimented doorways on the State House, constructed 1763 (left), and on the Third Meeting House, constructed 1757 (center). From a ca. 1830 painting by William Giles Munson.

[20] Doorway of the Capt. Charles Churchill house, Newington, Connnecticut. (photograph 1914-1916)

20. Newington: House of Capt. Charles Churchill (1723-1802).*

The date of this house is given variously as 1754 (*Wethersfield History*, 1:731) and as 1763 (Trowbridge, p. 319). The house was abandoned in 1887 and was much deteriorated by 4 July 1914 when rowdy boys blew up its center chimney (ibid.). The doorway, which was fitted to a six-inch overhang, was saved (WA since 1916). Photographs taken 1914-1916 (CHS) show that the gambrel-roofed house had a triangular pedimented side door and the interior work included two corner cupboards. The doorways and cupboards may have been constructed by the joiner Return Belden, brother-in-law of Capt. Charles Churchill.

Illustrated

Features: Ionic volutes surmounted by four petals in an X position in pilaster caps, small rosette on channelled keystone, six-point stars on rosettes at termination of scrolls, flame finial on a rectangular pedestal, double doors with X panels.

[20]   Capt. Charles Churchill house, Newington, Connecticut, built in 1754 or in 1763. (photograph after explosion of 4 July 1914 and before the doorway was removed in 1916)

21. Newington: House of Martin Kellogg, Jr. (1718-1791).†

An undated drawing (CHS) showing a large center-chimney, gambrel-roofed house with a scroll doorway is identified as the house of the Reverend Elisha Williams, minister of Newington from 1721 to 1726 and Rector of Yale College from 1726 to 1739. Previously published material (*Wethersfield History*, 1:764; Trowbridge, p. 159) indicates that the house was built 1720-1722 by the town for the minister and was acquired by Martin Kellogg, Sr. (1686-1753), when Williams moved to New Haven; but records do not support this, and clearly the house in the drawing is not a 1720s house. On 14 June 1720 Elisha Williams purchased seventy-nine acres with a house in present-day Newington from Jonathan Belcher, but the only Williams conveyance of land to a Kellogg occurred on 28 March 1757 when Elisha Williams, Jr., and Ezekiel Williams, executors of Elisha Williams, sold the same property with a dwelling house to Martin Kellogg [Jr.]. It seems likely that the house in the drawing was built by Martin Kellogg, Jr., after 1757 at which time the early house was either taken down or became the large kitchen ell as described by Trowbridge. The house remained in the Kellogg family until it burned in 1872. The drawing shows scroll pediments over the lower windows and triangular ones above on the front and side but does not show fluted pilasters with capitals reported to have decorated the front corners (Trowbridge, p. 159).

Features: (from drawing) double doors.

22. Northford: House of the Reverend Warham Williams (1726-1786).**

This house is said to have been built by Warham Williams in 1750 (Trowbridge, p. 249), the year he settled as minister in Northford. In 1979 the house was taken down and rebuilt on South Street, Roxbury, Connecticut. On the house are triangular window pediments with raised corners.

Features: six-petal rosettes in pilaster caps, duck-bill keystone, six-petal rosettes at termination of scrolls, finial missing but rectangular pedestal remains, rusticated surround, double doors.

23. Old Lyme: House of John McCurdy (1724-1785).**

This seventeenth-century house was remodelled about 1754, again altered in the nineteenth century, and was moved two times (Elmer D. Keith to AFM, 21 January 1960). John McCurdy, who bought and remodelled an early house, was married in 1752. According to Elmer Keith, ". . . the visible house is John McCurdy, 1754 . . . It has some of the richest 18th century panelling of that period." The scroll doorway, applied to a two-story enclosed porch probably of the first period, and triangular window pediments relate to the 1754 alterations.

Features: small, deeply carved six-petal rosettes in pilaster caps, keystone missing, deeply carved six-petal rosettes at termination of scrolls, finial missing from remaining rectangular base, double doors with X panels.

Old Lyme: Lloyd Hyde, see Hartford: House of Thomas Seymour (11).

24. Plymouth: Second Meeting House.

Two Barber drawings (CHS) show a scroll pediment over the main entrance of this meeting house built in 1790 (*Plymouth History*, p. 40).

25. Preston (Poquetanuck): St. James Church.

An ink and watercolor mourning piece (CHS), drawn by Hannah Punderson (ca. 1777-1821) about 1820 and completed after her death, shows monuments to Ebenezer Punderson (1735-1809) and his wife Prudence (Geer) Punderson (1736-1822). With penned inscriptions by two hands, these monuments are shown standing in a churchyard. On the right is a body of water with sailing vessels and on the left is a church with a scroll doorway on the side of the steeple and another indicated on the main steeple entrance. The water can be identified as Poquetanuck Cove; the church is St. James Episcopal Church, long associated with the Punderson family. Originally built in 1737 at North Groton, the church was moved in 1784 to a site at Shingle Point near the head of Poquetanuck Cove (Friary, p. 567). According to the following entry in Ebenezer Punderson's account book (CHS), a steeple was built at the new location 1786-1787: "1786 July 6th Jonª Brewster Esq. bet a case of gin, that there would be a Steeple finished with a Bell therein, to the Church on Shingle Point, in 12 months. . . ." The scroll doorways were probably constructed when the steeple was built. In 1841 the church was sold (Friary, p. 567). The site can still be identified.

Illustrated

Features: (from mourning piece) finial terminated with a cross, arched double doors.

[25] St. James Church, Preston, Connecticut, constructed 1737. The steeple, with a scroll pedimented doorway, was begun in 1786. From an ink and watercolor mourning piece by Hannah Punderson (ca. 1771-1821), begun in 1809 and completed about 1822 after her death.

[25]   St. James Church, Preston, Connecticut. Detail.

26. Roxbury: Meeting House.

Among the papers of the housewright David Fabrique and his brother Bartimus Fabrique, a joiner (Historical Records Collection, SLY), is an architectural drawing labelled "Plan for Roxbury Meeting House" that shows a scroll doorway. In 1795 the town of Roxbury was set off from Woodbury and a new meeting house was built in the center of the town (Crofut, 1:425). The Fabrique plan may not have been followed.

Features: (from plan) flame finial on high rectangular pedestal, probably double doors.

Roxbury: South Street, see Northford: House of the Reverend Warham Williams (22).

27. Southington: House of Samuel Curtiss (1737-1801). *†

Samuel Curtiss is said to have built this house in 1766 (NYHS *Quarterly* 42, no. 4, October 1958:403), the year of his marriage, on a lot that contained an earlier dwelling house according to land records traced by Abbott L. Cummings. In 1782 he sold it to the Reverend William Robinson. The house burned in January 1951, but the doorway and much of the interior were saved, purchased by Mrs. Katharine Prentis Murphy in the spring of 1951, and given to the New York Historical Society where the doorway was placed on display. (*Southington News*, 13 April 1951). There were triangular window pediments with raised corners on the house.   *Illustrated*

Features: double rosettes in pilaster caps and at termination of scrolls, keystone altered, doubled outline, width sufficient for former double doors.

28. South Windsor: House of Aaron Bissell (1737-1801).

Probably built about 1753 (Kelly, *Houses*, p. 110) or at least by the time of Aaron Bissell's marriage in 1757, the house, a tavern during the Revolution, was torn down in 1904 (Colonial Dames). The doorway, known from an early photograph (CHS), was saved but later burned in a barn (Colonial Dames, a pencil note).

Features: (from photograph) eight-petal rosettes in pilaster caps and at termination of scrolls, tapered keystone, panelled pedestal for cylindrical finial, doubled outline, double doors with X panels.

[27] Samuel Curtiss house, Southington, Connecticut, built about 1766. (photograph ca. 1925)

94200

FERNALD LIBRARY
COLBY-SAWYER COLLEGE
NEW LONDON, N.H. 03257

29. South Windsor: House of Ebenezer Grant (1722-1787).**

This house was raised on 23 June 1757 (Grant account books). The joiners and their pay were listed as: Gray £ 46-11-07, Aaron Grant £ 47-19-03, Abiel Grant £ 19-06-08, Josiah Vining £ 16-7-04, and Isaac Clark £ 2-9-03. A triangular pedimented doorway on the ell of the house has eight-petal rosettes in the pilaster caps. A side door on the house with a restored triangular pediment has ruffled pilaster caps.   *Illustrated*

Features: miniature scroll doorways on pedestals, foliage pilaster caps, small keystone incorporated by graduated fascia into entire entablature, no pulvinated frieze, six-point stars on rosettes at termination of scrolls, finial missing from remaining rectangular pedestal, doubled outline, double doors with S panels.

[29]   Ebenezer Grant house, South Windsor, Connecticut, raised 1757. (photograph ca. 1890)

[29]   Doorway of the Ebenezer Grant house. (photograph 1968)

30. South Windsor: Third Meeting House.

In 1757 the present town of South Windsor voted to build a new meeting house, and in 1761 it was further voted to build a steeple. The meeting house was seated in October 1761. In 1845 the meeting house was either moved or torn down (*Windsor History*, 1859, pp. 253-56). A nineteenth-century engraving of the meeting house (*Windsor History*, 1892, 1:729) shows a scroll pediment on the main door and one on the steeple door. The windows had triangular pediments. In 1761 the town owed £ 255-16-6 to Ebenezer Grant for purchasing materials. Abiel Grant, Alex Grant, and Aaron Grant, all joiners, were paid £ 68-16-2, £ 62-12-6 and £ 30-11-2 respectively (Grant account books).

Features: (from engraving) double doors with X panels.

31. Stratford: Christ Church.

The first service was held in this church on 8 July 1744, conducted by the Reverend Samuel Johnson; and the last, on 25 July 1858 (Wilcoxon, pp. 460, 473). The architect or designer was Thomas Salmon, a native of Chippenham in England who had immigrated to Stratford by 1720 (see Appendix II under Salmon, Thomas). But Salmon's name does not appear in church building accounts for receiving a major payment as would be expected. On a list of seventy-six church members who contributed funds to meet building costs, Salmon's name is also conspicuously absent (Orcutt, pp. 349-50); and perhaps it follows that Thomas Salmon's contribution was that of his service as architect.

In 1748 with work on the church still in progress, the Reverend Samuel Johnson commented that it was nearly finished and evaluated the edifice by declaring that "the architecture being allowed in some things to excede any thing before done in New England" (Wilcoxson, p. 455).

Two nineteenth-century oil paintings in the parish house of the present Episcopal church, one dated August 1857, testify to the truth of Johnson's statement. They show the church with a scroll doorway with arched double-leaf doors and a finial between the scrolls at the main entrance on the steeple. The paintings also show a triangular pediment on a side doorway of the steeple, triangular window pediments on the steeple, and on the main body of the church. Above the steeple was a graceful spire.

Until these paintings became known, knowledge of the appearance of the scroll pedimented doorway had been clouded by a nineteenth-century lithograph, a copy of which also hangs in the parish house. Drawn by W. Stanger of Bridgeport, but undated, the lithograph shows a large urn at the base of each scroll. Since these urns do not appear in either painting, but since each painting does show an urn at each corner of a balustrade on the steeple, the possibility exists that W. Stanger saw urns, formerly on the balustrade, lying about during or after the demolition and wrongly surmised that they belonged on the doorway. Or did the finial removed from between the scrolls confuse him?

At any rate, scroll pedimented doorways like the straightforward versions of the paintings were to be found nearby to Salmon in his youth in Chippenham, Wiltshire. In Corsham only five miles from Chippenham, he could observe several examples still surviving in stone on the High Street. Manneristic church monuments were also readily available to Salmon. Whether or not he

[31]   Christ Church, Stratford, Connecticut, begun 1743, demolished 1858. From an oil painting dated August 1857.

[31] Christ Church, Stratford, Connecticut. From an undated lithograph by W. Stanger, Bridgeport.

was ever within the walls of such great houses in Wiltshire as Longleat or Wilton House with its scroll pedimented overmantle in the celebrated Double Cube Room cannot be determined. Certainly Salmon was aware of arched double-leaf doors on both religious and secular buildings.

While the exact source for Salmon's design for the scroll pediment on Christ Church may never be known, the spire on the church appears remarkably similar to that on Wren's St. Martin Ludgate, 1677-1688, in London. Samuel Johnson was ordained at a St. Martin's church in London in 1723. Since James Gibbs's St. Martin-in-the-Fields was under construction from 1722 to 1726, the ordination likely occurred at St. Martin's on Ludgate Hill. That the spire of the Stratford church was based on St. Martin Ludgate is evident. The resemblance seems far from accidental but rather deliberately planned by the Reverend Samuel Johnson whose attachment to this particular church was probably of a personal nature.

If Salmon had not been acquainted with the Wren spire before his initial departure from England, he had ample opportunity to observe it in 1724 when, according to a letter of recommendation from the Reverend Samuel Johnson dated 11 June 1724, he journeyed to London (SPG, New England Letters #2, pp. 224-25, microfilm LC). In all likelihood Salmon was instructed by his minister to observe St. Martin Ludgate closely. Johnson quite possibly entertained ambitious plans for the first Episcopal church built in Stratford in 1723-1724.

Certainly Christ Church was an important building and an imposing structure in Stratford. The extent of influence carried by its scroll pedimented doorway in the Connecticut River Valley remains undetermined.   *Illustrated*

Features: Although the accuracy of the lithograph of Christ Church can be questioned on the basis of the two oil paintings — one dated August 1857 nearly a year before the church was pulled down — features of the doorway in the lithograph are included for sake of comparison; From paintings: high panelled pedestals, pilaster caps heavy and tapered downward, no keystone, modillions in cornice, high oval finial, possibly no surround, double doors arched at top; From lithograph: pedestals not panelled, fluted (and engaged?) columns with Corinthian capitals, undecorated keystone, no pulvinated frieze, petalled rosettes at termination of scrolls, no finial, large urns at base of each scroll, no surround, double doors arched at top.

32. Stratford: House of William Samuel Johnson (1727-1819).

A scroll doorway on this gambrel-roofed house can be seen on a nineteenth-century oil painting in the collection of the Stratford Historical Society. Said to have been built in 1739 by Paul Maverick and sold to David Brooks, the house was purchased by William Samuel Johnson in 1753 (Wilcoxson, p. 560); and it was probably he who made the improvements that included the addition of the doorway.

33. Stratford: House of David Judson (1693-1761).**†

The date 1723 traditionally assigned to this house has been revised to a later but undetermined year by Abbott L. Cummings. It was completed by 1758 when David Judson wrote his will. Above two doors on the house are heavy and projecting pediments. That over the front entrance is curved and supported by pilasters. Over the rear entrance stands an unsupported triangular pediment, which may have at one time been resting on consoles. Referring to these heavy pediments, Kelly noted, "This type of doorway appears to belong almost exclusively to Stratford" (Kelly, *Houses*, p. 106). Although relatively rare in eighteenth-century New England other than Stratford, similar heavy triangular pediments are not uncommon near Chippenham, Wiltshire County, England, former home of the Stratford joiner, Thomas Salmon. In the town of Corsham near Chippenham, such pediments are to be seen along the main street or the High Street. In all probability heavy projecting pediments were introduced to Stratford by Salmon, and those on the David Judson house are thought to be his work prior to his death in 1749 (see Appendix II under Salmon, Thomas).

In 1890, when a two-story porch was added to the front of the house, the pediment was placed in a gable of the porch while the lower part of the doorway remained in its original position. With the removal of the porch, the pediment was returned to its rightful place.

The house is now maintained by the Stratford Historical Society and is open to the public.   *Illustrated*

Features: pedestals not panelled, undecorated pilaster caps, no keystone, no pulvinated frieze, no finial, single door, rosettes at termination of scrolls eliminated by a raised horizontal piece joining the scrolls together.

34. Stratford: House of Robert Walker, Jr. (1705-1722), no pediment.**

Oak-framed, this house was built, according to a marker, in 1690 by Zachariah Booth. In 1727 Robert Walker purchased the lot with a house for his son Robert Walker, Jr., who was probably the actual builder of the present dwelling. Later he added a scroll doorway and elaborate interior panelling. The latter remains, but the pediment was removed probably when a porch was placed at the front entrance. In 1919 a photograph of the house with its double overhang and porch was published with the following caption: "One is tempted to believe that the door itself and the fluted pilasters of the doorway, along with such elements of a scroll pediment as are still visible beneath the very much later added porch, were applied when the windows were changed" (*White Pine*, February 1919, pp. 11-12). In 1934 the house was moved from Main Street to 2175 Elm Street, and the porch was removed; but the pediment was not restored. Gen. Joseph Walker, by whose name the house was once known, was a son of Robert Walker, Jr.

Features: panelled pedestals (restored), fluted pilasters, undecorated pilaster caps and keystone, pulvinated frieze, single door, no elements of a scroll pediment now visible.

35. Suffield: House of Seth Austin (1731-1806).

About 1900 this house, formerly on Main Street, was torn down and the ell was

[33] David Judson house, Stratford, Connecticut, showing eighteenth-century pediment preserved in gable of Victorian porch. (photograph 1890s)

moved to Bridge Street (*Suffield Anniversary*, p. 175). The scroll doorway, seen on old photographs (CHS), was most likely destroyed with the house. Seth Austin probably built the house about 1754, the year of his marriage.

36. Suffield: House of the Reverend Ebenezer Gay (1718-1796).**

This gambrel-roofed house was raised on 11 April 1743 and was first occupied on 14 November 1743 (Gay memoranda). However, the doorway, if original to the house, was probably constructed at a later date. Although a photograph of about 1905 (AHS, Howes negative) shows the doorway on the house as it is now, there are indications that it has been narrowed, which raise questions concerning the origin of the doorway. The window above the doorway is shorter than other second-story windows, possibly having been altered to accommodate a pediment. In 1933 the house was purchased by Suffield Academy.

Features: panelled pedestals (restored), undecorated pilaster caps, no keystone, narrow pulvinated frieze, eight-petal rosettes at termination of scrolls, no finial, rusticated surround (inside only), single door with X panel.

[37]   Doorway of the Joseph Pease house, Suffield, Connecticut. (photograph ca. 1920)

37. Suffield: House of Joseph Pease (1728-1794).

This gambrel-roofed house was raised on 24 July 1760 and was finished in 1762 (Pease diary). The scroll doorway, known from early photographs (CHS and SPNEA), was probably built in those years and appears to be the work of John Steel, Jr., and Oliver Eason, documented builders of the Samuel Colton doorway in Longmeadow, Massachusetts (Eason died in 1761). The house was torn down in 1902 (*Suffield Anniversary*, p. 169). In 1959 Charles Bissell of Suffield stated that the doorway had been sold to someone in Ohio. On the house were a triangular pedimented side door and triangular window pediments with elm tree devices, possibly the work of Parmenas King whom Joseph Pease would have known before he moved from Enfield to Suffield in 1750 (ibid., p. 167).

Illustrated

Features: (from photographs) pedestals replaced, foliage pilaster caps, fish-scale or thumbprint keystone, multi-petal rosettes at termination of scrolls, rectangular pedestal for missing finial, doubled outline, rustication around door only, not outside, double doors with X panels.

[37] Joseph Pease house, Suffield, Connecticut, raised 1760. (photograph ca. 1915)

38. Suffield: Third Meeting House.

Known from Barber sketches (CHS), a scroll doorway was the main entrance to this meeting house, which was raised 8 to 12 May 1749 (Gay memoranda). There were also a triangular pediment on the steeple door and triangular window pediments. In 1835 the meeting house was replaced with a new one (*Suffield Anniversary*, p. 139).

39. Waterbury: House of Capt. George Nichols (1714-1786).

Built by Capt. George Nichols about 1760, this house was next owned by his son, John Nichols. It stood on East Main Street; and although greatly altered in 1865, it was still standing in 1896 (*Waterbury History*, 2:346-47) but has since been removed. The scroll doorway and house are shown in nineteenth-century drawings in *Waterbury History*.

Features: (from drawings) rosettes in pilaster caps, tapered keystone, pinwheel rosettes at termination of scrolls, pineapple (?) finial on rectangular pedestal, width sufficient for former double doors.

40. Waterbury: Third Church.

A nineteenth-century drawing from memory of this church by an unknown artist shows a scroll pediment on the steeple doorway. The church was begun in 1796 and was used until 1840 (*Waterbury History*, 1:614).

41. Wethersfield: House of Simeon Belden (1737-1820).**

The date of this gambrel-roofed house is uncertain and has been given as both 1760 (*Wethersfield Doorways*) and 1767 (John C. Willard to AFM, 25 November 1959). Simeon Belden married in 1765. The scroll doorway was probably contemporary with the house. Purchased in the nineteenth century by Comstock, Ferre & Co., the house has had only minor exterior alterations. In 1917 when the doorway was restored, the pedestals, then missing, were replaced as were the double doors (Willard letter). The house has triangular window pediments with raised corners.   *Illustrated*

Features: six-petal rosettes in pilaster caps, duck-bill keystone, six-petal rosettes at termination of scrolls, mushroom finial on rectangular pedestal, rusticated surround, double doors (not original).

42. Wethersfield: House of Joseph Boardman (1695-1771).

This house stood at the southwest end of Broad Street (*Wethersfield History*, 2: facing p. 116). A nineteenth-century painting of it, owned by William F.J. Boardman in 1904, shows a scroll pedimented doorway and triangular window pediments. Both may have been added to an earlier house as Samuel Boardman (1648-1720) is said to have built this house for his son Joseph Boardman in 1719 (ibid.). The house was destroyed in either 1857 or 1866 (ibid., 1:726).

Features: (from painting) double doors.

[41]   Simeon Belden house, Wethersfield, Connecticut, built ca. 1765. (photograph 1968)

43. Wethersfield: House of Samuel Boardman (1648-1720).

A nineteenth-century drawing of this house shows a gambrel-roofed house with a scroll pedimented doorway that stood on Broad Street until 1827 when it burned. The house is said to have been built in the early eighteenth century and to have remained in the family until it was purchased in 1816 by Hezekiah Crane who kept tavern there (*Wethersfield Doorways*). An earlier house may have been altered or replaced by Samuel Boardman (1744-1822), grandson of the early Samuel, who inherited the property from his uncle David Boardman.

44. Wethersfield: House of Col. John Chester (1703-1771).

A nineteenth-century drawing, captioned "The Col. John Chester House," shows a scroll doorway. The caption also tells that the house was located on the west side of Broad Street, that it was built about 1710, that all the materials were brought from England, and that the house was demolished in 1869 (*Wethersfield Doorways*). The house with its double overhang may have been earlier than the doorway, but more likely both dated to the marriage of John Chester in 1749. Certainly all the materials were not imported.

Features: (from drawing) double doors.

45. Woodbury: Second Meeting House.

Built in 1746-1747, this meeting house was in use until 1818 when a new one was seated. A nineteenth-century engraving (*Woodbury History*, 2:942) shows a scroll pediment over the main entrance and one over the steeple entrance.

[46] Rosette at termination of scrolls. Doorway of Capt. Thomas Dickinson house, Deerfield, Massachusetts.

Massachusetts

Boston: MFA, see Hatfield: House of Elihu White (56).

Boston: MFA, see Longmeadow: House of Samuel Colton (57).

Boston: State Street Trust, see Hatfield: House of Jonathan Allis (52).

46. Deerfield: House of Capt. Thomas Dickinson (1718-1814).**†

Evidence beneath clapboards above the present flat-top doorway indicates the presence of a former pediment on the Capt. Thomas Dickinson house, built about 1760 as indicated by purchases of building materials (Williams, Elijah account books). Fragments of a scroll pediment, donated to the PVMA museum by Charles Jones, a late nineteenth-century owner of the house, and believed by him to have once been on the Fourth Meeting House, are stylistically correct for remaining decoration on the doorway. The pediment was probably removed prior to 1847 when Jones purchased the house. Aware that the meeting house did have a scroll pediment, Jones, who probably found the fragments in his barn or attic, made an incorrect assumption concerning the origin of his fragments. Among the Jones fragments is a rectangular finial. The meeting house, however, had a mushroom finial, which is also in the PVMA museum. Clearly the presence of two finials implies two scroll pediments.

Features: (on house) foliage pilaster caps and keystone, doubled outline, rusticated surround, width sufficient for former double doors; (in museum) rosettes formerly at termination of scrolls contain four double-leaf petals, rectangular finial with six-petal rosette on rectangular pedestal.   *Illustrated*

Deerfield: Dwight Barnard House, see Springfield: House of Josiah Dwight (60).

47. Deerfield: Fourth Meeting House.

Built in 1729 and torn down in 1824, this meeting house underwent major repairs in 1768 that included the building of a steeple at the north end. A drawing of the building made from memory by Nathaniel Hitchcock, who was twelve in 1824, shows a scroll pedimented doorway at the main entrance, a triangular pediment on the steeple door, and triangular window pediments (Meeting House file, PVMA library). These probably all relate to the 1768 remodelling. The mushroom finial from the scroll doorway survives (PVMA museum).

Features: (from drawing) fluted pilasters, rosettes in pilaster caps and at the termination of the scrolls, mushroom finial on rectangular pedestal, double doors.

48. Deerfield: House of Elijah Williams (1712-1771).**†

When this house was threatened with destruction in 1877, successful efforts to save it leaned heavily on the argument that it was the house built by the town in 1707 for the Reverend John Williams who had been taken captive to Canada in 1704. To promote interest in the house, the Deerfield historian George Sheldon wrote articles that appeared in the Greenfield *Gazette and Courier* on 2 July, 30 July, and 6 August 1877, all suggesting that the 1707 house had survived having undergone extensive repairs in the 1750s by Elijah Williams, son of the minister. Actually Elijah Williams, who had resided in Enfield, Connecticut, from 1747 to 1751, did have work done on his father's house following his mother's death on 21 June 1754. On 5 December 1754 the joiners Parmenas King, who had accounts with Elijah Williams in Enfield, and Oliver Eason were credited with thirty-seven and thirty days' work respectively by Williams (Williams, Elijah account books). However, it is apparent from Elijah Williams's accounts that he built a new house in 1760 and pulled down the old one. Williams purchased twenty-nine loads of stone (for a cellar) in February 1760 and subsequently lumber, lath, lime, and brick. He also paid for labor throughout the year, sold eleven old window frames, and on 4 September credited Samuel Partridge with £ 39-0-2 for "work at my house." This work probably included the scroll doorway. The house also has a triangular pedimented side door and triangular window pediments with raised corners.

Illustrated

Features: six-petal rosettes in pilaster caps, fluted keystone, six-petal rosettes at termination of scrolls, mushroom finial on rectangular pedestal, doubled outline, rusticated surround, double doors with X panels.

[48]   Maj. Elijah Williams house, Deerfield, Massachusetts, built 1760. (photograph ca. 1910)

[48] Doorway of the Elijah Williams house, Deerfield, Massachusetts, constructed 1760. (photograph 1930s)

49. Hadley: House of Eleazer Porter (1698-1757). †

Descending to Eleazer Porter from his father, Samuel Porter (1660-1722), this homelot, the southern of two adjacent Porter lots on the east side of Hadley's town common, had a house standing on it in 1709 when the estate of Samuel Porter's mother was distributed. Eleazer Porter lived on this lot until his death when it became the property of his son Elisha Porter (1742-1796). Known only from photographs probably taken in the early 1880s (privately owned, copies AFM), the house is difficult to date. A Whitefield drawing (SPNEA) shows a center chimney house and gives the date 1714. However, neither the drawing nor later photographs show an overhang like that on the Porter house next north. Whatever the period of construction, it was probably Elisha Porter who arranged for the scroll doorway, possibly in 1761 when his brother Eleazer Porter (1728-1797) is believed to have commissioned a similar doorway in anticipation of his marriage on 13 May 1762. In 1870 the house descended to Pamela, a granddaughter of Elisha Porter, who had married Dudley Smith. In 1960 Frank Reynolds of Hadley reported to AFM that in 1887 an entry in his mother's diary noted that the house was being pulled down. The structure is generally known as the Elisha Porter house.

[50]   Samuel Porter house, Hadley, Massachusetts. The house, with a hewn overhang, was built before 1722; the doorway was added about 1761. (photograph 1934)

50. Hadley: House of Samuel Porter (1660-1722).** †

In 1709 when his mother's estate was settled, Samuel Porter inherited two adjacent homelots on the east side of Hadley's town common, each with a house standing on it. In his will he left all of his property to be divided between his sons Samuel Porter (1685-1748) and Eleazer Porter (1698-1757). The northern lot went to Samuel, whose son Moses Porter sold it to Samuel's brother Eleazer Porter in 1749. When Eleazer Porter died, a 1758 inventory listed two houses, "House & Homestead £ 333-6-8 D⁰ £ 300-0-0." A 1762 deed for abutting property indicates that Eleazer Porter, Jr. (1728-1797), son of Eleazer, was living on the northern lot. The lot remained in the Porter family until 1866. The house, which still stands, has a hewn second-story overhang with carved corner posts and is clearly an early house. It was probably built before 1722 by Samuel Porter whose inventory listed a parlour chamber, hall chamber, parlour, hall, kitchen, kitchen chamber, and cellar. A Whitefield drawing of the house (SPNEA) gives the date 1713. The scroll doorway adapted to the overhang may have been commissioned by Eleazer Porter, Jr., about the time of his second marriage on 17 September 1761. The death of Anna Porter, widow of his uncle Samuel Porter, on 11 May 1761 gave Eleazer Porter, Jr., full title to the property for the first time. The dwelling is generally known as the Eleazer Porter house.

Illustrated

Features: foliage pilaster caps and keystones, rosettes at termination of scrolls contain four double-leaf petals, foliage decorated rectangular finial on rectangular pedestal, doubled outline, double doors with X panels.

Hatfield.

(Of the six scroll pedimented doorways known to have once stood in Hatfield, only one remains, that on the Simeon Wait house. The Elihu White doorway has been at the MFA since the 1930s. The four others are known only from early photographs labelled Hatfield. These four were sorted out and identified in

1958 by the Misses Marion and Louisa Billings of Hatfield, now deceased, who were able to recognize the houses and doorways and to supply names of owners within their memories. Subsequent title searches made it possible to determine eighteenth-century owners. The Misses Billings also supplied dates when houses were moved and taken down.]

51. Hatfield: House of Eleazer Allis, Jr. (1725-1781), pediment only.* †

An early photograph of the Eleazer Allis, Jr., house, labelled only Hatfield (GHS), shows a pitched-roof, center-chimney structure with a scroll pediment over the front door. Although most other features are indistinct, both scrolls appear in need of repair; the finial is missing, and the entire doorway below the scrolls has been removed. Identified by the Misses Marion and Louisa Billings in 1958 as the McHugh house formerly on the east side of Main Street, it was also known to them as the house of Remembrance Bardwell, a house erroneously said to have been built on the original John Wells lot. That the builder was Samuel Hastings is also an error (*Hatfield History*, pp. 269, 302-3). A title search indicated that the lot was originally owned by Samuel Gillet, that it was owned by both Remembrance Bardwell and Samuel Hastings in the nineteenth century, and that it was purchased by John McHugh in 1864. Land records also show that the property with a house on it was sold by Samuel Gillet to Eleazer Allis in 1753 for £173. It was probably Eleazer Allis who built the house shown in the photograph, although he may only have added the doorway to the house he purchased. The house was torn down in 1904; and in 1910 when the *History of Hatfield* was published, "the scroll and casing" of the front door were reported to be preserved in Hatfield's Memorial Hall (p. 302). When a search of this building was made in 1958, no fragments of any doorway were to be found. Not recalling that the scrolls of this doorway were ever placed in Memorial Hall, the Misses Billings reported that in 1919 there was a fire in the post office where early furniture and architectural objects were housed, and that following the fire many surviving items were moved about and subsequently sold.

In the 1920s Lewis N. Wiggins of Northampton was actively collecting in the area "bricks, paneling, boards, doors, and a wide assortment of utensils taken from old houses. . . ." (*Northampton Book*, p. 369). When in 1927 he became the first manager of the newly completed Hotel Northampton, he purchased the adjoining building, furnished it with his collection, and opened Wiggins Old Tavern. A post card (AFM) dated 1927-1928 from automobiles in the foreground shows a scroll pediment set inside an entrance with a round-headed glass-paned top on the south side of the hotel. This pediment was generally known to have had a Hatfield origin. The entrance was replaced about 1976 by a plate glass bay window.

In 1982 Norman and Mary Gronning of White Creek, New York, placed a scroll pediment over the front door of the Isaac Stratton house in South Williamstown, Massachusetts. The finial, entablature, pilasters, and entire lower part of the doorway are of recent construction, based largely on the Stockbridge doorway of the Reverend John Sergeant house. The pediment, which was purchased by the Gronnings in 1980, was identified on the basis of comparison with photographs as the pediment from the side door of the Hotel

Northampton, which in turn was probably the pediment once on the Eleazer Allis house in Hatfield.

Features: (from photograph) only scrolls and rosettes at termination of scrolls remain; (from post card) scrolls and rosettes affixed to a backing with low circular cutouts to reveal glass in round-headed window behind, a tall finial, probably a pineapple, reaching far above the scrolls; (from Isaac Stratton house) scrolls and rosettes affixed to same backing as in post card, all now backed again by boarding to conceal clapboarding, six-petal rosettes at termination of scrolls with small circular indented centers, pineapple finial removed, newly made finial, scrolls and finial resting on a dentil course of old material applied by Norman Gronning, all below dentil course newly made.

52. Hatfield: House of Jonathan Allis (1721-1797), pediment only. * †

Land records indicated that in 1749 Eleazer Allis (1677-1758) deeded his homelot with "buildings thereon" to his son Jonathan Allis. On this homelot on the east side of Main Street, there stood a house with a scroll pediment until it was moved to Upper Lane before 1869. An undated photograph (SPNEA) shows only a view of the scroll doorway, not of the entire house. Only the pediment of the doorway survived at the time the picture was taken. After 1917 the house was torn down; a notation on the photograph states that in 1924 Leonard Goulding of South Sudbury, Massachusetts, was storing the pediment for Wallace Nutting. In a letter to AFM of 12 August 1959, Mr. Goulding confirmed this but stated that he did not know who did the restoration work. Although records do not disclose the date of purchase, the restored pediment with a newly made lower portion was acquired by the State Street Trust Company, Boston. Jonathan Allis may have built a new house on his father's homelot or he may merely have added the scroll doorway. It is also possible that both house and doorway were conveyed in the 1749 deed, but this seems unlikely.

Illustrated

Features: (of pediment, before restoration, from photograph) foliage keystone, pulvinated frieze, rosettes at termination of scrolls contain four double-leaf petals, rectangular finial on rectangular foliage decorated pedestal (both now replaced), doubled outline, width sufficient for former double doors.

53. Hatfield: House of Reuben Belding (1718-1778). †

Land records indicate that in 1753 John Belding deeded a part of his homelot with no buildings upon it to his son Reuben Belding. Soon after he received his land, Reuben Belding probably built the house now known from a photograph taken about 1900 (GHS). He probably also pulled down the old house belonging to his father next door that he inherited in 1758. A title search indicated that the old house was built before 1710 and was not therefore the house in the photograph constructed in a later period with a scroll doorway and triangular window pediments. In 1778 Reuben Belding's house became the property of his nephew Silas Porter when the Belding estate was distributed. In 1913-1914 the house on the east side of Main Street was torn down.

Features: (from photograph) width sufficient for former double doors.

[52] Doorway of the Jonathan Allis house, Hatfield, Massachusetts, constructed ca. 1760. (photograph before demolition of the house in 1917)

[55]   Doorway of the Simeon Wait house, Hatfield, Massachusetts, constructed in the 1760s. (photograph 1968)

54. Hatfield: House of Elijah Dickinson (ca. 1733-1813). †

Known from an early photograph (privately owned, copy AFM), this house on the west side of Main Street was torn down in 1892. Land records show that Elijah Dickinson purchased the lot with a house from his father Obadiah Dickinson in 1764 for £ 187-13-4 and that Obadiah Dickinson had purchased the same property in 1751 for the same price. Obadiah Dickinson had made no improvements on the house in the years of his ownership. The scroll doorway was probably added by Elijah Dickinson about the year he purchased the house. The triangular window pediments relate to the period of the doorway.

Features: (from photograph) six-petal rosettes in pilaster caps, fluted keystone, six-petal rosettes at termination of scrolls, mushroom finial on rectangular pedestal with a six-petal rosette on panel, rusticated surround, width sufficient for former double doors.

55. Hatfield: House of Simeon Wait (b. 1716). ** †

According to land records, Simeon Wait purchased this property in 1742 for £ 75-15 and sold it in 1772 for £ 186-13-4. He may have torn down the house he bought and rebuilt as the 1742 price does not suggest a particularly ambitious house. The scroll doorway and triangular window pediments were probably the work of Samuel Partridge in the 1760s. *Illustrated*

Features: six-petal rosettes in pilaster caps, fluted keystone, six-petal rosettes at termination of scrolls, mushroom finial on rectangular pedestal, rusticated surround, double doors (not original; double doors at foot of steps to cellar beneath a bulkhead on the south side of the house are probably the original doors).

[55] Simeon Wait house, Hatfield, Massachusetts, constructed in the 1760s. (photograph ca. 1905)

[56]   Elihu White house, Hatfield, Massachusetts, built about 1762. (photograph ca. 1910)

56. Hatfield: House of Elihu White (1734-1794).* †

Before 1931 Wallace Nutting gave the doorway of this hipped-roof square house to the MFA whose records date the house as 1762, the year of Elihu White's marriage to Zerviah, only child of Ebenezer Coles. A title search indicated that Ebenezer Coles purchased a five-acre homelot on the north side of Elm Street in 1736, and although no conveyance has been located, it appears that Ebenezer Coles deeded a half interest in this lot to his son-in-law Elihu White. Ebenezer White (1766-1826), son of Elihu, kept tavern in the house and left it to his son Horace White. In 1858 John T. Fitch and George C. Fitch acquired the property. About 1861 John T. Fitch moved the house to the rear of the lot to be used as a tobacco warehouse and built a new house (*Hatfield History*, p. 314).

Illustrated

Features: pedestals missing, vine-carved pilasters, tulips and rosettes in pilaster caps, foliage keystone, rosettes at termination of scrolls contain four double-leaf petals, mushroom finial on rectangular pedestal, doubled outline, rusticated surround, double doors (probably not original).

[56]   Doorway of the Elihu White house.
(undated photograph, as installed in the
Museum of Fine Arts, Boston, in 1921)

[56]   Carved pilaster capital. Doorway of
the Elihu White house. (photograph 1983)

[57]   Doorway of the Samuel Colton house, Longmeadow, Massachusetts, constructed 1754 by John Steel, Jr., and Oliver Eason. (photograph after 1921 installation in the Museum of Fine Arts, Boston)

[57]   Samuel Colton house, Longmeadow, Massachusetts, built in the 1750s. (photograph before 1916 when the doorway was removed)

57. Longmeadow: House of Samuel Colton (1727-1784).*

From Colton's account books it appears that work was being done on his house during the 1750s. On 24 June 1754 Colton credited "Olever Eson & John Steel 2 [Jr.] Work Don at a Dore. . . ." Eason worked about thirty-four days and Steel, twenty-eight. Only the elaborate scroll pedimented front doorway on Colton's house could account for this amount of labor. On 20 July 1754 Parmenas King contracted to do all other joinery work on the east side (front) of the house. This work would have included the triangular window pediments with raised corners and elm tree devices in the centers. One window pediment survives at SPNEA. The gambrel-roofed house was torn down in the summer of 1916 (*OTNE* 7 December 1916:19-20) and by 1921 the doorway had been installed in the MFA (MFA *Bulletin* 19 October 1921:57).   *Illustrated*

Features: delicate leafy pilaster caps, fishscale or thumbprint keystone, quatrefoil-like rosettes at the termination of the scrolls with pendants hanging from rosettes (right rosette and pendant restored), flame finial on a rectangular pedestal (both now replaced), doubled outline, rusticated surround, double doors with X panels with a rare segmental panel at top.

58. Northampton: House of Lt. Caleb Strong (1710-1776). †

Land records indicate that in 1745 Jonathan Strong gave the eastern two acre half of his homelot to his son Caleb Strong, which included the "Easternmost Dwelling House." Caleb Strong, father of Gov. Caleb Strong, may have either torn down this easternmost house and rebuilt or have made improvements on it about 1754, the traditional date assigned the gambrel-roofed house. The house with a scroll doorway and triangular window pediments, known from a photograph of a daguerreotype (FoL), was moved from the corner of Main Street and Strong Avenue to Pleasant Street about 1850 (*Northampton Homes*, pp. 16-17). On 31 August 1911 notice was given that it was to be torn down (*Hampshire Gazette*).

59. Pittsfield: House of the Reverend Thomas Allen (1743-1810).

This house and doorway, known from early photographs (property of the *Berkshire Eagle*), were probably constructed shortly after the Reverend Thomas Allen became the minister at Pittsfield in 1764. When the house was taken down on 1 November 1859 (*Pittsfield Sun*, 10 November 1859, p. 2), it was located on the corner of East and First streets.

Features: (from photographs) width sufficient for former double doors.

South Williamstown: Isaac Stratton House, see Hatfield: Eleazer Allis, Jr., house (51).

60. Springfield: House of Col. Josiah Dwight (1715-1768). * †

Land records indicate that when Josiah Dwight purchased a homelot on the west side of the main street in Springfield in 1743, there was a house standing on the lot. The house was built by David Ingersol who purchased an unimproved lot in 1723 and sold the same lot in 1733 with a house, reserving rights to the downstairs for his mother, the widow Ruth Ingersol, during her lifetime. Following her death in 1747, Josiah Dwight was free to either build a new house or to alter and improve the old one. (A strong case for the latter has been made by Robert St. George, "The Dwight Barnard House"). Accounts in the day book of Josiah Dwight indicate that by 1755 construction work was underway. Dwight paid for bricks, mortar, sill work, setting glass, putty, boards, and shingles. On 5 December 1755 Dwight credited the joiner John Steel, Jr., for two window frames. The scroll doorway was probably constructed about 1755 and because of stylistic affinity to the documented doorway on the Samuel Colton house, Longmeadow, Oliver Eason and John Steel, Jr., are suggested as the joiners. The triangular window pediments with raised corners and elm tree devices also resemble those on the Colton house known to be the work of Parmenas King.

In 1829 Howard Street was opened on the southern boundary of the Dwight homelot; and at some as yet undetermined date between 1865 and 1886, the house was moved around the corner to face Howard Street. In 1924 the doorway was purchased by Henry Francis du Pont from Charles Woolsey Lyon and according to Mr. du Pont was installed at his home in Southampton, Long Island (AFM interview with Ruth Betts, Winterthur, Delaware, April 1962). Subsequently the doorway was moved to Mr. du Pont's home at Winterthur.

In 1951 the Dwight house was moved to Deerfield where a reproduction of the doorway, then not known to be at Winterthur, was made by Francis Olszewski of South Deerfield, based on early photographs (SPL) that show it on the house.

Illustrated

Features: pedestals replaced, multi-petal rosettes in pilaster caps, multi-petal rosettes at termination of scrolls, flame finial on tall rectangular pedestal, doubled outline, rusticated surround, double doors with X panels.

[60] Josiah Dwight house, Springfield, Massachusetts, enlarged 1755. (photograph ca. 1920)

[62] Ephraim Williams house, Stockbridge, Massachusetts, built 1750-1760. From a nineteenth-century drawing.

61. Stockbridge: House of the Reverend John Sergeant (1710-1749).**

According to tradition this house, also known as the Mission House, was built about 1739, the year in which the Stockbridge minister married Abigail Williams. There is a local legend that the doorway was made in Westfield and transported to Stockbridge by ox team (*Mission House*). Actually this doorway closely resembles those of the 1760s attributed to Samuel Partridge and may have been done by him after 1757 when Sergeant's widow and her second husband Gen. Joseph Dwight moved to Great Barrington leaving the house to Sergeant heirs. (General Dwight's brother, Seth Dwight of Hatfield, was Partridge's father-in-law.) The possibility exists that the entire house was built by heirs of the Reverend John Sergeant after 1757. In 1928 the house was acquired by Mabel Choate who moved it from its original site on the hill above the center of Stockbridge to the main street; in 1948 ownership was transferred to the Trustees of Reservations.

Features: foliage pilaster caps, fluted keystone, rosettes at termination of scrolls contain four single-leaf petals, a finial of Ionic volutes stands on a foliage decorated pedestal, rusticated surround, double doors with X panels.

62.   Stockbridge: House of Col. Ephraim Williams (1691-1754).

In the Historical Room at the library at Stockbridge is an unsigned, undated drawing of a house with a scroll doorway and also a rosette fragment formerly at the termination of a scroll. Both are labelled "The Ephraim Williams House." Ephraim Williams, one of the original settlers of Stockbridge, built the house in 1750 according to the label. Constructed of black oak and surrounded by a moat, the house served as a fort during the French and Indian War (Abbott, pp. 232-33). The house stood on the hill north of the present town street and when the Reverend Stephen West, who was ordained as minister of Stockbridge in 1759, married Elizabeth daughter of Ephraim Williams about 1760, the house became their residence (*Stockbridge History*, p. 162). The scroll doorway may have been added by Stephen West. In 1850 the house was torn down by the Reverend Henry M. Field who built a new house on the old foundations.
Illustrated

Features: (from drawings) indications of vine-carved pilasters, double doors; (from rosette fragment) four double-leaf petals.

63.   Westfield: House of Daniel Fowler (1729-1801). * †

In 1916 the MMA purchased a scroll doorway that had been removed from a house in Westfield according to the seller, Charles Woolsey Lyon (MMA file). It was once thought to have been on the tavern of Ezra Clapp, but an early photograph (Crawford, p. 334), showing the doorway on the gambrel-roofed house standing at the corner of Main and Exchange streets and known to have been the tavern of Daniel Fowler, has removed any confusion: the doorway at the MMA was previously at the front entrance of Daniel Fowler's house. A title search indicated that in 1916 when Mary Schaefer, then owner of the house, died, her estate was handled by a public administrator who sold the house to Nelson B. Richardson on 1 July 1916. It was likely during this period of transition that the doorway was sold to Lyon.

Land records further show that Daniel Fowler purchased two adjacent parcels of land fronting north on the present Main Street in Westfield. In 1751 he purchased 2½ acres with "house, shop, Barn & other Small Buildings," and in 1760 he bought an additional 1½ acres adjoining and to the west of the first parcel, "with the buildings thereon." That Daniel Fowler built his gambrel-roofed house on the 1760 purchase and removed the house he bought in 1751 is made evident when by 1814 a total of 3 acres had been sold off the east end of the homelot, leaving the house on a small parcel at the west.

Alexander Grant who moved from South Windsor, Connecticut, to Westfield about 1764 may have worked on the doorway as may have Ahimaz Eason who moved to Westfield from Suffield, Connecticut, about 1762. An unidentified person with the initials S.F. stated, "The ornamental work around and over the front door [of the Fowler house] my father said took a man a month's work" (*Westfield History*, 1:568). A reproduction of the original doorway was placed on the house in 1980.
Illustrated

Features: miniature scroll doorways on pedestals, foliage pilasters, foliage pilaster caps, tapered keystone, rosettes at termination of scrolls replacements, cylindrical finial on rectangular foliage pedestal, doubled outline, rusticated surround, double doors with S panels.

64. Westfield: House of Azariah Moseley (1735-1791). †

Known from an early photograph labelled "The Azariah Moseley Place — Silver Street" (*Picturesque Hampden*, p. 79), this house had been moved to the back of its lot by 1900 (*Westfield Souvenir*, p. 26) and was later torn down. It had triangular window pediments.

New York

New York: MMA, see Westfield, Massachusetts: House of Daniel Fowler (63).

New York: NYHS, see Southington, Connecticut: House of Samuel Curtiss (27).

65. Unknown location: unknown house.

An early but unidentified photograph (SPNEA) shows a pitched-roof and center-hall house with a scroll pediment and triangular window pediments. (Those on the side of the house may have had elm tree devices in the center.) Although features of the doorway are indistinct, general proportions of the house and architectural details suggest a Connecticut River Valley origin.

[63]   Doorway from the Daniel Fowler house, Westfield, Massachusetts, constructed
ca. 1762, purchased 1916 by the Metropolitan Museum of Art. (photograph as installed
at the MMA before replacement of rosettes in 1958)

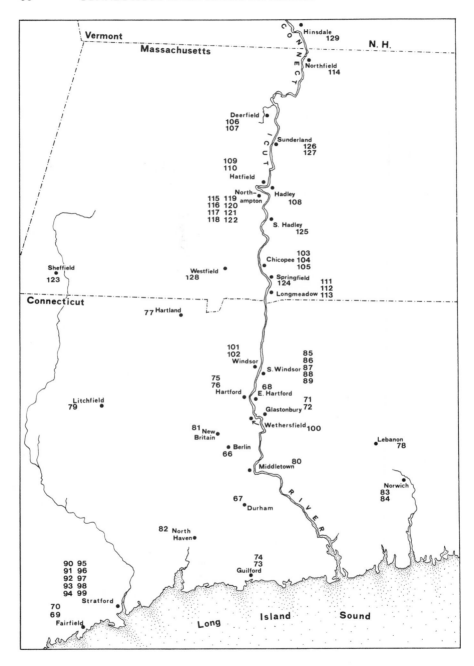

Figure 4   Distribution of triangular pedimented doorways in the Connecticut River Valley.

Triangular Pedimented Doorways

Connecticut

66. Berlin: House of Lt. Joseph Beckley (1695-1772).

Early photographs (CHS) labelled "Beckley House, Berlin 1658" show a triangular pedimented doorway on a house with a roof damaged by fire. A Whitefield drawing of about 1882 (Whitefield, *Connecticut*) prior to the fire is captioned, "This was formerly a tavern, and Washington is said to have stopped here. It is believed to be about 175 years old." More likely the house was built by Joseph Beckley about the time of his first marriage in 1750.

Darien: on Arrowhead Way, see Northampton, Massachusetts: House of William Parsons (120).

67. Durham: House of the Reverend Elizur Goodrich (1734-1797).**

The date 1763 for this house is based on family tradition among the descendants of Elizur Goodrich who resided in the house until recent times. Although the triangular pediment of the doorway was removed in the nineteenth century when a front porch was constructed, an early photograph (privately owned, copy AFM) shows a former pediment, which has been reproduced. The house with a double overhang has triangular pediments on the gable windows. Goodrich, who was a native of Wethersfield, may have employed a joiner from that town to work on the doorway.

Features: undecorated pedestals, eight-petal rosettes on pilaster caps, truncated keystone, doubled outline, double doors (not original but reproduced on basis of photograph).

68. East Hartford: unidentified house.

A photograph of about 1890-1900 (CHS) labelled only "East Hartford" shows a center-chimney house with a pitched roof and a triangular pedimented doorway on the front of the house. Efforts to identify the house have been unsuccessful.

Features: (from photograph) base of pilasters missing, single door.

69. Fairfield: Court House.

A Barber drawing of this courthouse (CHS), built after Fairfield was burned in 1779, shows a triangular pediment on the main doorway.

70. Fairfield: Fifth Meeting House.

A Barber drawing of this meeting house (CHS), built in 1785 after Fairfield was burned in 1779, shows a triangular pediment on the main door and on the steeple door.

71. Glastonbury: House of Sgt. John Hollister (ca. 1642-1711).

A drawing published in 1886 (*Hartford County History*, p. 208) shows a triangular pedimented doorway on the front and side, both adapted to overhangs. The house is said to have been built in 1675 (*Hartford County History*, p. 208). If so, the doorways were later additions.

72. Glastonbury: House of Capt. Nathaniel Talcott (1678-1758).

A drawing published in 1886 and labelled "the Talcott Home, 1699" (*Hartford County History*, p. 209) shows a house with triangular pedimented doorways on the front and side and triangular window pediments. A casement window with diamond panes surviving over the front door argues for the early date. (The window is in the collection of the Glastonbury Historical Society.) If the house was built in 1699, the pediments were added later. In 1904 the house was standing and was still in the Talcott family (*Wethersfield History*, 2:696).

Greenwich: unknown location, see Hadley, Massachusetts: House of Aaron Cook (108).

73. Guilford: House of Ezra Griswold (1753-1814).**

Sources differ as to the date of this house. J. Frederick Kelly (*Houses*, p. 135) gives a date of 1760 for "the Ezra Griswold house," which if built by Ezra Griswold cannot be correct. Records of the Colonial Dames (CSL) list the same house as the George Griswold house and state that the house was built by Ezra Griswold about 1777 or soon after, but this date may be based on the 1777 marriage of Ezra Griswold. The doorway closely resembles the doorway on the Samuel Robinson house (74) with an unverified date of 1752, suggesting that the house may have been built in 1760 by Thomas Griswold (1708-1784), father of Ezra. The doorway with fluted pilasters and pulvinated frieze qualifies only as a peripheral example of the Connecticut River Valley style.

Features: pedestals missing, undecorated pilaster caps, no keystone, wide single door.

74. Guilford: House of Samuel Robinson (1725-1802).

An early but undated photograph (SPNEA) shows a doorway nearly identical to the one on the Ezra Griswold house (73), but in addition to fluted pilasters this doorway has panelled pedestals, a keystone, and a frieze composed of a cyma curve. In the 1930s the date 1752 was to be seen in the pediment (Chamberlain, *Doorways*, p. 50). Samuel Robinson married in 1760. The house was demolished in 1937 (Colonial Dames).

Features: (in addition to the above) undecorated pilaster caps, wide single door.

75. Hartford: House of John Lawrence (ca. 1719-1802).

This doorway is known from a nineteenth-century print (CHS) labelled "Old Lawrence Mansion, Hartford. John Lawrence, Treasurer of Conn. 1769-1789 . . . Built in 1785."

76. Hartford: Saunder's Old Tavern.

A photograph of a nineteenth-century drawing (CHS) shows a house with triangular pediments over the front and side doors and over the windows. It is labelled "Saunder's Old Tavern and Tree on South side of Charter Street."

77. Hartland: Meeting House.

A Barber sketch of a meeting house labelled only "Hartland" (CHS) shows a triangular pedimented doorway. A meeting house was built in 1771 in East Hartland and in 1780 in West Hartland (Crofut, 1:297).

78. Lebanon: House of Gov. Jonathan Trumbull (1710-1785).**

According to the autobiography of the artist John Trumbull, his grandfather Joseph Trumbull (1678-1755) "acquired a fine new home in Lebanon in 1740"; and it is generally believed that the present house was built in that year. However, during restoration work in 1960 evidence was uncovered to indicate that the original house was small (Warren, *Fitch*, p. 41). Entries in the account books of Jonathan Trumbull (CHS), who moved into the house when his father died, refer to work on his "new" house, meaning his father's house — new to him. From 1762 to 1767 work was being done. On 29 January 1763 Ebenezer Bacon sold Jonathan Trumbull "200 Squares of Glass for ye New House." On 8 February 1763 Trumbull recorded a credit, "Isaac Bayler Junr . . . by hearth Stones & getting stones for my New House 8-6-0." In March 1763 Ebenezer Fitch was credited for "Boardg the Joiners, Masons & others at Work on my house." The doorway can safely be considered a part of the 1760s renovations. The house has triangular window pediments.

Features: panelled pilaster caps, no keystone, double doors.

79. Litchfield: House of Gov. Oliver Wolcott (1726-1797).

A marker on this house states that it was built in 1753, which was two years prior to Wolcott's marriage. A portico of about 1800 probably replaced an earlier doorway whose pilasters remain. The house has a triangular pedimented side door with ruffled pilaster caps and triangular window pediments with raised corners. The original pediment over the front door may not have been triangular; there may have been at one time a scroll pediment.

80. Middletown: House of Philip Mortimer (ca. 1710-1794).

A Whitefield drawing (Whitefield, *Connecticut*) entitled "The Mortimer House, Middletown, Conn." shows a triangular pedimented doorway and triangular window pediments. The caption for this gambrel-roofed house states: "This, in its best days, was a very fine place on high ground, overlooking the Connecticut River, with an avenue of splendid trees, but is now going fast to ruin. It was built by Philip Mortimer, about 1750."

81. New Britain: House of Capt. Josiah Lee (b. 1711).

Known from an early photograph (CHS), this house with a triangular pedimented doorway adapted to a front overhang is said to have been built for Josiah Lee by his father Stephen Lee about 1740 and to have later become the residence of the Reverend Newton Skinner. The house stood on East Street in 1888 (reverse of photograph). The doorway may have been added about 1766 when Elizabeth Lee, daughter of Josiah, married John Patterson.

Features: (from photograph) pediment had raised corners and a four-leaf pinwheel in the center of the triangle, width sufficient for former double doors.

82. North Haven: House of the Reverend Benjamin Trumbull (1735-1820).**

Located at 11 Trumbull Place on the east side of the green, this house with a triangular pedimented doorway and triangular window pediments with raised corners was built by the minister in 1761 with timber "out of the Societies lot" (Crofut, 2:644). A history of the house written in 1923 (Colonial Dames) refers to a building expense list for May 1761 in the Reverend Benjamin Trumbull's account book but does not give the location of the book.

Features: eight-petal rosettes in pilaster caps, keystone largely missing, sufficient width for former double doors.

83. Norwich: House of Joseph Carew (1738-1818). †

A house with a triangular pedimented doorway standing on East Town Street is shown in a photograph published in 1895 (*Norwich Houses*, p. 256). Land records indicate that Joseph Carew purchased part of the original Simon Huntington lot in 1763 with only a shop on it. He probably built the house in anticipation of his marriage in 1765. The house has recently been confused with that of Jacob Perkins (*Norwich Homes*, p. 27). Joseph Trumbull was a later owner of the house.

84. Norwich: House of Joshua Prior, Jr. (bp. 1746).**†

According to land records, Joshua Prior, Jr., purchased a lot in 1759 from Joshua Norman. He probably built his house prior to his marriage in 1762. The house was later designated as 407 Washington Street. The doorway qualifies only as a marginal example of the Connecticut River Valley style.

Features: short pedestals with full-length pilasters, raised rosettes in pilaster caps, undecorated keystone, broken or open triangular pediment, double doors.

85. South Windsor: House of John Hoskins, Jr.?

An early photograph (SWL) shows this house with a triangular pedimented doorway and triangular window pediments. It is labelled, "Built on the Gov. [Roger] Wolcott farm in 1752. Bought by Enoch W. Pelton in 1859. Taken down in 1898." From another source Enoch W. Pelton is said to have owned the Ephraim Wolcott house, which stood on part of the original Gov. Roger Wolcott farm. Inside the house "upon an attic-beam is nailed a piece of board, marked 'A.W. 1752' which has been supposed to be the date of its erection" (*Windsor History*, 1892, 1:773). The same account states that Ephraim Wolcott inherited the house from some cousins "of the name of Hotchkiss, or Hoskins." Land records show that on 8 May 1747 Roger Wolcott sold land to John Hoskins, Jr., on which the latter probably built the house in question. It is not known whether Ephraim Wolcott (1714-1762) or his only son Ephraim Wolcott, Jr. (1762-1826), inherited the house from Hoskins.

Features: (from photograph) fluted pilasters, rosettes in pilaster caps.

86. South Windsor: House of Matthew Rockwell (1707-1782).

Old but undated photographs (SWL) show a house without a chimney and falling to ruins. It had a triangular pedimented doorway and was identified as the Henrietta Rockwell house, built by Matthew Rockwell before 1750. Matthew Rockwell was married in 1743.

Features: (from photographs) rosettes in pilaster caps, single door.

87. South Windsor: House of Timothy Strong (1719-1803).

A 1920s photograph of a frame house with brick ends and identified as a house built by Timothy Strong about 1753 (Kelly, *Houses*, p. 20, pl. 4) shows a triangular pedimented doorway and also triangular window pediments. Timothy Strong married his first wife in 1753. His son David Strong was the next owner. The house was torn down after 1894 by Frank B. Rockwell (Colonial Dames).

88. South Windsor: House of Nathaniel Strong (1712-1795).**

Although tradition holds that this house was built in 1698 by Jacob Strong (Colonial Dames), it was more likely built by his son Nathaniel Strong about the time of his marriage in 1747. In addition to the triangular pedimented front doorway, the house has two side doors with triangular pediments, one on the main house and one on the ell, which appear to be authentic though not necessarily original to the house. Mr. Ben Bancroft, owner in 1959, said that the side doors were added in 1918; but he did not know where they came from. *Features:* pedestals restored, undecorated pilaster caps, keystone covered by later door frame, single door.

89. South Windsor: House of Gov. Roger Wolcott (1679-1767).

A nineteenth-century drawing of this house shows a triangular pedimented doorway. Built probably in the 1750s, the house was torn down about 1830 (*Windsor History*, 1892, 1:773-74).
Features: (from drawing) single door.

90. Stratford: House of Capt. James Booth (1734-1809).

This house on the south side of Essex Place is said to have been built by James Booth, a carpenter and builder, in 1757, the year of his marriage. The doorway, known from a photograph (Wilcoxson, p. 336), may have been added about 1765-1775 according to Raymond D. Cable of Devon, Connecticut. Mr. Cable also stated that the doorway and other woodwork as well as the center chimney were removed in the 1930s, and at that time the house was covered with stucco.

91. Stratford: House of John Brooks (1715-1777). **

Although this house at 2288 Main Street is said to have been built by William Wilcoxson in 1715, it was probably enlarged by John Brooks who purchased the property in 1746 (Wilcoxson, p. 616). David Brooks was a later resident.
Features: tall fluted pilasters on short bases, six-petal rosettes on pilaster caps, diminutive keystone, double doors.

92. Stratford: House of Nathaniel Curtis (d. 1761). **

This house, formerly on lower Elm Street, was built about 1735 (Wilcoxson, p. 698); but the doorway was probably a later addition since the window over the triangular pediment has been reduced in size. In 1973 the house was moved to 600 Housatonic Avenue.
Features: tall fluted pilasters on short bases, undecorated pilaster caps, double doors.

93. Stratford: Fourth Congregational Church.

When the fourth meeting house was built in 1786, its dimensions and general appearance were similar to those of the third meeting house that burned in 1785. An undated engraving, possibly made prior to the demolition, shows a triangular pediment on the main door, the front steeple door, and on the side door of the steeple. The meeting house was taken down in 1858 (Wilcoxson, pp. 136, 409).

94. Stratford: House of Stiles Judson (1752-1834).

Known from early photographs (Wilcoxson, p. 514), this house with a triangular pedimented doorway was torn down many years ago according to local residents. A post card in the possession of Raymond D. Cable indicates that the house was standing in 1911. The house is said to have been built in 1778 for Stiles Judson who married in 1777.

95. Stratford: House of John Patterson (1711-1806).

Although this house is said to have been built by Robert Clark about 1670, it was greatly altered and enlarged by John Patterson who owned it from 1745 to 1753. The triangular pediment, known from an old photograph (Wilcoxson, p. 668), was probably added by John Patterson. During the nineteenth century the house was owned by the Dayton family and is known by the name of the Dayton house. It was torn down in 1915 (Wilcoxson, pp. 669-71).

Features: (from photograph) a heavy, possibly unsupported, pediment, single door.

96. Stratford: House of Josiah Peck (1751-1821).

Said to have been built in 1774 by Nathan Peck for his son Josiah, this house with a triangular pedimented doorway, known from an early photograph, was remodelled in 1885 and later torn down to make space for a fire station (Wilcoxson, p. 158).

Features: (from photograph) double doors.

97. Stratford: House of Abraham Thompson (1721-1774).

This house, which stood on the east side of Elm Street, was built in 1742 when the lot was given by Thomas Thompson to his son Abraham, then about to be married. In 1794 the house was sold to Isaac Pendleton, and it was owned by that family until it was torn down in 1890. The triangular pediment is known from an early photograph (Wilcoxson, p. 496).

Features: (from photograph) a heavy, possibly unsupported, pediment, single door.

98. Stratford: House of Dr. Agur Tomlinson (1720-1774).**

Built in 1772, this house formerly stood on the site of the Stratford Library. It was moved in 1895 to 2272 Elm Street where it has been restored. An early photograph (Wilcoxson, p. 520) shows a triangular pediment over the front door, which has since been replaced by a triangular pedimented portico possibly incorporating the early pediment.

Features: (from photograph) a heavy pediment; (on house) tall fluted pilasters on short bases, six-petal rosettes in pilaster caps, a band of narrow dentils across frieze, double doors.

99. Stratford: House of Col. Joseph Wooster (1702-1791).

This house, which stood on the north side of Far Mill River, was built about 1750 and burned in 1914. The triangular pediment is known from an early photograph (Wilcoxson, p. 430).

100. Wethersfield: House of Maj. Josiah Griswold (1701-1769).

A nineteenth-century drawing (*Wethersfield Doorways*) of this gambrel-roofed house formerly at Griswoldville shows triangular pediments over the front and side doorways and over the windows. Although the reverse of a photograph of the house taken prior to demolition (WHS) states that it was built in 1726 (the year prior to the marriage of Josiah Griswold) and torn down in 1860, the house has features of the 1750s or 1760s. The doorways may have been constructed by Return Belden, brother-in-law of Josiah Griswold. The house descended to Josiah Griswold's grandson, another Josiah Griswold (1771-1802), whose widow married Samuel Broadbent (1759-1828).

101. Windsor: House of Henry Allyn (1699-1753).

A nineteenth-century sketch of a house labelled "View of Old Squire Allen's house in Broad Street Windsor Conn" (CHS) shows an early house with an elaborate stacked chimney and a triangular pedimented doorway. This house was built by Henry Allyn, who married in 1728, and was later lived in by his son Henry Allyn, Jr. (1728-1804). The doorway was certainly of a later date than the house.   *Illustrated*

[101]   Henry Allyn house, Windsor, Connecticut, built ca. 1728 with a doorway added at a later date. From a nineteenth-century drawing.

[102] North Society Meeting House, Windsor, Connecticut, built 1762. (photograph 1933)

102. Windsor: North Society Meeting House.

A house of five bays with a triangular pedimented doorway and triangular window pediments on both the first and second floors stood at 531 Palisado Avenue in 1933 but has now disappeared. A photograph dated 1933 (WiHS) identifies the building as the North Society Meeting House, 1762-1793, and gives the 1933 address.   *Illustrated*

Massachusetts

103. Chicopee: House of Abel Chapin (1700-1772).

Known from an early photograph (*Chicopee Street*, facing p. 16), this house, said to have been built about 1730, had a triangular pedimented front door. A Whitefield drawing of the house (SPNEA) gives the date 1740. Maj. Moses Chapin (1762-1834), a later owner, was a grandson of Abel Chapin.

104. Chicopee: House of Col. Abel Chapin (1756-1831), no pediment.*

An 1890s photograph of this gambrel-roofed house known as the Chapin Tavern gives the date 1785 (*Chicopee Street*, facing p. 48). Other views taken in the 1920s (SPNEA) give excellent details of the doorway. This doorway, without a pediment, was sold by Steve Racz of Milford, Connecticut, to Hollis S. Baker in 1953. With a newly made scroll pediment added, the doorway was placed at the entrance to the Baker Museum for Furniture Research, Holland, Michigan. A few years after this sale a front porch was torn off the house and traces of a former triangular pediment were found.

Features: (from photographs) short pedestals, Ionic volutes in pilaster caps, no keystone, no pulvinated frieze, double doors.

105. Chicopee: House of Seth Chapin (1724-1806).

An early photograph of this house (*Chicopee Street*, facing p. 37) gives the date 1793 and shows a triangular pediment. Zerah Chapin, whose name is associated with the house, was a son of Seth Chapin. The photograph is indistinct, and the triangular pedimented doorway may be of a more federal style than the earlier Connecticut River Valley doorway.

106. Deerfield: House of John Sheldon (1710-1793).**†

Land records indicate that in 1734 when John Sheldon purchased the lot on which this house stands, there were no edifices on it; but he probably built the present house shortly after his purchase. He married in 1735. Wind braces in the attic and other structural features substantiate the early date. However, the doorway seems related in style to the triangular pedimented side doorway on the Elijah Williams house of 1760 in Deerfield. Triangular window pediments on the two houses are similar as well, suggesting that about 1760 John Sheldon added exterior trim to his house. While not so narrow as the thirty-four-inch single side door on the Williams house, the doors on John Sheldon's house are exceptionally narrow for double-leaf doors, each measuring about twenty-one inches. Although the narrow doorway conforms more nearly than any other known to proportions recommended by Edward Hoppus in *The Gentleman's and Builder's Repository* (2d ed., London, 1738), the explanation for such narrow proportions is likely to be purely practical. John Sheldon's original front door was probably a single door, constructed in the 1730s before the fashion for double doors had taken hold. Dealing with a predetermined space and probably taking into account that the facade of the house as a whole was also narrow, the joiner, possibly Samuel Partridge, avoided the structural undertaking of widening the entire opening and yet permitted John Sheldon to enjoy fashionable double doors.   *Illustrated*

Features: pedestals replaced (restoration based on an 1890s photograph of the house, PVMA library), six-petal rosettes in pilaster caps, undecorated keystone, narrow double doors.

[106] Doorway of the John Sheldon house (Sheldon-Hawks), Deerfield, Massachusetts, constructed about 1760 for a house of about 1734. (photograph ca. 1910)

107. Deerfield: Eaglebrook School, pediment only.*

A triangular pediment, presently on a house at the Eaglebrook School with a newly made lower portion, was probably removed in the 1930s from its now unknown original location.

Features: duck-bill keystone, undecorated pilaster caps, raised corners in the pediment, width sufficient for former double doors.

108. Hadley: House of Aaron Cook (1699-1779).**†

A Whitefield drawing of this house (SPNEA) identifies it as the John Cook house and gives the date 1760, but the center-chimney house with a front overhang and five windows on the facade may have been built about 1733 by Aaron Cook who was deeded a half acre out of the homelot of his father Westwood Cook in that year. When John Cook (1726-1805), a son of Aaron Cook, married in 1760, he may have added the doorway. John Cook inherited his father's house that stood on the south corner of the road leading from the common to the burying ground. In 1950 William E. Gass of South Deerfield dismantled and moved the house to Greenwich, Connecticut. Photographs taken during the dismantling are in the files of Historic Deerfield, Inc.

Features: (from photographs) double doors.

109. Hatfield: House of Dr. Waitstill Hastings (1714-1748).†

Land and probate records indicate that Waitstill Hastings probably built a house between 1742 and 1748, the year of his death. In 1742 he purchased sixteen acres of land with buildings for £250. An inventory of 1749 appraised the same homelot at £3500. Although 1749 was a period of inflation, the significant rise in value of the property suggests that a house was built. The house stood at the south end of Hatfield's main street on the east side and was inherited by John Hastings (1738-1811), son of Waitstill. About 1880 the house was moved by a descendant, Howard Abbott, who told AFM in 1959 that he used the old house for storing onions. Since 1959 the building has been torn down. According to Mr. Abbott, the doorway, known from an early photograph (Howard Abbott, copy AFM), may have been sold to a bank in Waltham long before the house was moved; but efforts to locate it have been unsuccessful.

Features: (from photograph) double doors.

110. Hatfield: House of Lt. Moses Graves (1700-1785).†

Land records indicate that in 1737 Moses Graves purchased unimproved land from his father, Jonathan Graves, and that in 1768, following his move to Pittsfield, he sold his homelot with a house to William Williams (1735-1808), son of Col. Israel Williams whose large gambrel-roofed house on the main street was torn down in 1857 (*Hampshire Gazette*, 14 March 1907, "Old Hatfield Houses"). An etching (SPNEA) dated 24 June 1881 and inscribed "Old Williams House Hatfield, Mass." shows a house with a pitched roof, a center chimney, and a triangular pedimented doorway. This house can be identified as the William Williams house that stood near the old burying ground. Later the house was occupied by Israel Williams, Jr. It burned before 1909 (*Hatfield History*, p. 283).

Features: (from etching) double doors.

111. Longmeadow: House of Simon Colton (ca. 1711-1796).**†

When John Colton died the town of Longmeadow was a part of Springfield. According to land records, his estate was divided in 1734; and his fourteen-acre homelot in "the Field Called Longmeadow Field" was awarded to his son Simon Colton who married in 1736. Simon Colton may have built a new house on his father's homelot in 1734 as indicated by a marker on the house, although the marker is probably based on the date of the inheritance. The house and doorway may well have been constructed slightly prior to 1757 when the Hampshire County Court of General Sessions first granted a tavern license to Simon Colton. The house was long known as the Old Red House.

Features: low unpanelled pedestals, undecorated pilaster caps, single door.

112. Longmeadow: House of Thomas Hale (1672-1750).

When this house was taken down in 1893, a board was found inside the chimney with the date 5 April 1705 (LmHS, file on old houses). If the board was not reused, this date may indicate the year when the house was built. Thomas Hale was married in 1705. The doorway, known from an old photograph (*Longmeadow Sesquicentennial*, called Willard House, 260 Longmeadow Street), was probably added by Thomas Hale, Jr. (1705-1797), who inherited the house. Or Thomas Hale, Jr., may have torn down his father's house and built a new one.

113. Longmeadow: Second Meeting House.

Raised 18 June 1767 (Colton account books), this meeting house stood on the common and had, according to an early photograph (*Old-Time Meeting Houses*, facing p. 104), three triangular pedimented doorways and triangular window pediments, all with elm tree devices in the center. Parmenas King, who made similar pediments for the Samuel Colton house in Longmeadow, was paid for work on the meeting house (Colton account books). In 1884 the meeting house was moved and greatly altered (LmHS). None of the pediments can now be found.

Features: (of main doorway from photograph) elm tree device in pediment, double doors.

114. Northfield: Second Meeting House.

This meeting house was raised in 1762 and was torn down in 1833. A sketch published in 1875 shows a triangular pediment over the main door and also on the front and side of the steeple (*Northfield History*, pp. 311-16).

Features: (from sketch) double doors.

115. Northampton: House of Ebenezer Clapp (1726-1797).**†

Research on this house indicated that it was probably built by Ebenezer Clapp shortly after he inherited the property from his father, Samuel Clapp, in 1761. Standing at 148 South Street, the house was restored by Karl S. Putnam, an architect of Northampton, who sold it to the Betty Allen Chapter of the Daughters of the American Revolution in 1926. Putnam told AFM that when he purchased the house there was a porch over the front door, although pilasters from an early doorway remained. Evidence of a former triangular pediment appeared when the porch was removed. The present pediment was designed by Karl Putnam.

Features: fifteen-petal rosettes in pilaster caps, duck-bill keystone, wide single door, all work above the architrave is restoration.

116. Northampton: House of Capt. Roger Clapp (1684-1762).†

A Whitefield watercolor (SPNEA) labelled "Built by Capt Roger Clapp 1713" and "South St. Northampton" shows a house with a front overhang, a center chimney falling in ruins, five windows across the front (that over the front entrance considerably smaller than the others), a leanto, and a triangular pedimented front doorway adapted to the overhang. In 1848 Simeon Clapp (b. 1759), grandson of Roger Clapp, also gave the date 1713 (*Hampshire Gazette*, 10 November 1885, "Old Landmark Gone."), a date compatible with the outward appearance of the house. Simeon Clapp further recalled that the leanto was added when he was young. The doorway was probably also added in the 1760s. Referred to in nineteenth-century land records as the "Warham Clapp homestead," the house was sold to George Ellsworth in 1857. In 1885 Ellsworth sold it to Dwight A. Horton who tore down the old house. On 16 September 1921 the property at 215 South Street was acquired by the Lathrop Home for Aged and Invalid Women to replace the first home across South Street on the Samuel Edwards, Jr., homelot (205).

117. Northampton: House of Luther Clark (1767-1855).†

Land records supply the history of this house with a triangular pedimented doorway known from an old photograph (FoL). In 1792 Daniel Pomeroy sold unimproved land to Luther Clark who probably built a house on it soon after and who added a small parcel of land in 1801 and another in 1807. In 1809 Solomon Stoddard (1771-1860) purchased the property with a house on it from Luther Clark. The house remained in the Stoddard family until 1861. In 1880 it was purchased by Smith College and was later torn down. The southern wing of the Smith College Alumnae House was built on the site.

118. Northampton: House of Maj. Timothy Dwight (1726-1777).†

According to tradition this house was built by Timothy Dwight in 1751 (*Northampton Homes*, p. 19), the year after his marriage. The property, as indicated by land records, came to the Dwight family in 1745 through Timothy Dwight's mother, Experience King, daughter of John King. Located on King Street opposite Park Street, the house became the rectory for the Catholic church in 1905 and has since been torn down. Although early photographs (FoL) indicate that a nineteenth-century porch either obscured or caused the removal of the original front doorway, the large gambrel-roofed house is included here because of other features seen in the photographs, namely a triangular pedimented side door and triangular window pediments both with elm tree devices, and a scroll pedimented dormer window, the center of three on the gambrel roof.

Illustrated

[118]   Maj. Timothy Dwight house, Northampton, Massachusetts.

119. Northampton: House of Isaac Parsons (1715-1798). †

In 1914 this house, then thought to be the oldest still standing in Northampton, was torn down (*Hampshire Gazette*, 4 April 1914). Said to have been built for Isaac Parsons in 1744 at the time of his marriage (*Parsons House*, p. 32), the house is shown in old photographs (FoL) with a triangular pedimented doorway. According to land records, Josiah Parsons gave land and buildings to his son Isaac Parsons in 1761. The gift was to include "all that part of my Home lot which he the said Isaac has lately and now improves and Dwells upon with all the buildings and Edifices. . . ." The house stood on Parsons Lane near the cemetery.

Features: (from photographs) single door.

120. Northampton: House of William Parsons (1690-1768) pediment only.** †

Probate records indicate that William Parsons, who inherited the homelot and house of his father John Parsons in 1728, probably pulled down the old house and built a new one slightly prior to 1756 when he wrote his will leaving the house to his only son, Samuel Parsons (1733-1812). By 1765 when he added a codicil, a new ell had been completed. In the codicil William Parsons provided for his only surviving daughter, Margaret, "the use and improvement of my North Great Chamber in the front of my House and the Improvement of a Back Room in the New House & Kitchen & Cellar. . . ." Samuel Parsons married in 1768, the year of his father's death, and may have altered the house to its gambrel-roofed form before selling it to Ebenezer Lane in 1788. In 1935 Herbert P. Luce purchased the front or gambrel-roofed part of the house, then at 392 Bridge Street, for $3,400 and employed Steve Racz of Milford, Connecticut, to move it to Arrowhead Way, Darien, Connecticut. Photographs taken about 1935 (FoL) show that when Mr. Luce purchased the house there was a portico at the front entrance, but stretching across the top of a door and an adjacent window on the left side of the house was a triangular pediment that was of sufficient size to have once stood over the front door. (*Living With Antiques*, p. 149, shows the pediment on the side of the house.) During restoration after the house was moved, this pediment was returned to the front entrance, and other elements of the doorway were newly made. Both the doorway pediment and those on the windows have elm tree decoration. In the north chamber, left for the use of Margaret Parsons, are pilasters with foliage decorated caps and miniature scroll doorways in the pedestals.

Features: none known with the exception of the pediment with an elm tree device.

121. Northampton: House of Sgt. Jonathan Strong (1708-1797).†

Known from two photographs, one dated 20 September 1926 and labelled "Northampton, Mass. Strong House" (FoL) and the other labelled "Old House, South Street, Northampton" (GHS), this house was built by Jonathan Strong possibly at the time of his marriage in 1730. The house had a center chimney (in need of repair when the photographs were taken), a double overhang, a pitched roof with a leanto, nine windows on the front, and a triangular pedimented doorway adapted to the front overhang. In 1774 Jonathan Strong gave the north half of his homelot, which included the house, to his son Jonathan (1737-1803). A third Jonathan (1773-1855), grandson of Sergeant Jonathan, built a new house on the property in 1799, just north of the old house. The old house remained in the family until 1922 when all but the 1799 house was sold to a developer, and Harlow Street was cut through the lot. The old house was probably torn down shortly after the 1926 photograph was taken.

122. Northampton: unidentified house.

A photograph of about the 1880s showing a house with a triangular pedimented doorway and filed with Northampton residences at the Forbes Library is labelled, "Clapp house Cor. South Street & Columbus Ave. Present site of Frank Clapp house." At some later date the following was added, "wrongly titled This was not Clapp hse. K.S. Putnam." Karl Putnam, a Northampton architect who resided on South Street, was correct. The eighteenth-century Clapp family house on the east corner of South Street is not the house in the photograph; nor did the house built by Frank L. Clapp in 1904 (*Northampton Buildings* #1046) on the west corner replace it. The center-chimney house in the photograph has nine windows across the front, and the window above the front entrance is shorter than other upper windows as if altered to accommodate the triangular pediment added at a later date. This house cannot be located on South Street or elsewhere in Northampton. It may have been torn down soon after the photograph was taken.

123. Sheffield: House of Col. John Ashley (1709-1802).**

In 1959 Mr. Edward Brewer, then owner of the house, stated to AFM that he recalled a brick marked 1735 that was uncovered in 1930 when the house was moved from its original site across the road on the present Route 7A. The brick has since been lost. The style of the doorway suggests a date in the 1760s or later, and the doorway appears similar to the side door on the circa 1760 Gen. Joseph Dwight house in nearby Great Barrington (190). Now the property of the Trustees of Reservations, the house has exceptionally fine panelling in the two front upstairs rooms.

Features: full-length pilasters on short pedestals, undecorated pilaster caps, duck-bill keystone, single door.

124. Springfield: House of Jonathan Dwight (1743-1831). †

According to the caption on an early photograph (*Springfield Sketches*, p. 177), this house originally stood on the west side of Main Street opposite State Street and was moved about 1840 to 53 State Street. Land records indicate that Jonathan Dwight who married in 1766 purchased part of Jonathan Day's former homelot, without a house, from his uncle Josiah Dwight in 1768. The photograph shows a triangular pediment with elm tree decoration.

125. South Hadley: Second Meeting House.

An oil painting by Joseph Goodhue Chandler (1813-1880?), a native of South Hadley, shows a triangular pediment over the front or main door and another on the steeple (*Old-Time Meeting Houses*, facing p. 74). There also were triangular window pediments. The meeting house was built in 1761, but the steeple was not added until about 1792. In 1826 the house was remodelled and in 1844 it was torn down (*South Hadley*, pp. 114-18).

126. Sunderland: House of Abner Cooley (1713-1788). *

Abner Cooley, first settler of the Plumtrees section of Sunderland, built a two-story house with a triangular pedimented doorway in 1758 that was torn down by Charles Cooley, grandson of Abner. When Charles Cooley constructed a brick house across the road in 1821, he saved the doorway and placed it on the frame ell of the new house (*Springfield Union*, 14 May 1939).

Features: fluted pedestals, fat moldings between pedestals and upper pilasters missing but outlined in paint, undecorated pilaster caps and keystone, width sufficient for former double doors.

127. Sunderland: Second Meeting House.

Built 1792-1794, this meeting house has been greatly altered; however an undated drawing shows that it once had a triangular pediment over the front door and on a side door of the steeple (*Sunderland History*, facing p. 54, p. 56).

128. Westfield: House of Thomas Ingersoll (1692-1748). †

A nineteenth-century photograph (WeA) shows a basic center-chimney house with five windows across the front and a triangular pedimented doorway. On the right side of the house a two-story ell can be seen. An inscription on the photograph states that the house was built in 1698 by John Ingersoll and that it burned in 1890. Another source states, "A memorandum in the hands of Maj. Ingersoll, at the United States Armory, says that this house was built by Thomas Ingersoll, Esq. who was a magistrate, and died in 1748" (*Connecticut Valley History*, 2:943). Probate records indicate that Thomas Ingersoll left his real estate to be divided between his sons Jonathan (1715-1755) and John (1731-1792). John Ingersoll, who married in 1752, may have added the doorway and also the ell.

Michigan

Holland: Baker Museum, see Chicopee, Massachusetts: House of Col. Abel Chapin (104).

New Hampshire

129. Hinsdale: House of Col. Ebenezer Hinsdale (1703-1763).**

This house is said to have been built in 1759 by Col. Ebenezer Hinsdale of Deerfield, Massachusetts, the founder and first settler of Hinsdale (*Cheshire County Homes*, p. 29). The doorway, the only known example of the true Connecticut River Valley style north of Greenfield, was probably constructed by a joiner from Massachusetts.

Features: six-petal rosettes in pilaster caps, thumbprint decoration on keystone, doubled outline, width sufficient for former double doors.

Vermont

130. Newbury: House of Col. Thomas Johnson (1742-1819).**

On the east side of Route 5 north of the center of Newbury stands a house whose front and side entrances both have elements reminiscent of the Connecticut River Valley style. Nearby a historic marker indicates that the house was built by Thomas Johnson when he settled in Newbury in 1762. However, according to another source (*Newbury History*, p. 587), Thomas Johnson who was born in Haverhill, Massachusetts, apparently built three houses, the first in 1766, another in 1775, and a third in 1800. The house near the marker may be the latter.

Features: full fluted pilasters, pinched or mild hourglass shaped pilaster caps, pulvinated frieze, single door.

131. Rockingham: Second Meeting House.**

According to town records, this meeting house was built in 1787. The main entrance and also the porch entrances have triangular pedimented doorways with elements of the eighteenth-century Connecticut River Valley style.

Features: fairly high undecorated pedestals, fluted pilasters, undecorated pilaster caps, compressed entablature including pulvinated frieze, modillions in cornice and pediment, double doors.

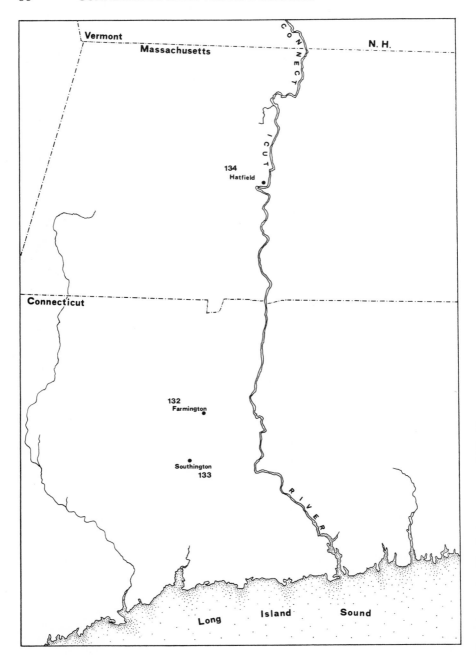

Figure 5   Distribution of segmental pedimented doorways in the Connecticut River Valley.

Segmental Pedimented Doorways

Connecticut

132. Farmington: House of John Thompson III (1704-1775).**

Built by Judah Woodruff on a lot purchased by John Thompson in 1769, this house at 17 Main Street was moved back from the street in 1920 at which time the center chimney was removed (Farmington Catalogue). The doorway was adapted to a shallow front overhang.

Features: raised foliage on pilaster caps, simple geometric design on keystone, applied finial ascending in two points, double doors with X panels (possibly not original).

133. Southington: House of Elisha Root (1737-1776).**†

According to land records, two houses stood on property purchased by the brothers Elisha and Amos Root from Joseph and Samuel Cogswell in 1762; however, only one house stood on the lot in 1764 when Amos Root sold his share to Elisha. Between 1762 and 1764 Elisha Root had probably torn down the two houses and built the present one in anticipation of his marriage in 1764. The doorway, adapted to a shallow front overhang, is probably contemporary with the house.

Features: lacy notches above fluting on pilaster caps and keystone, three six-petal rosettes connected by lacy notches in the pediment, double doors (not original).

Massachusetts

134. Hatfield: House of John Dickinson (1707-1799).**†

In 1747 John Dickinson (1667-1762) gave the lot on which this house stands to his son Thomas Dickinson who according to the unrecorded deed (Dickinson Papers, PVMA library) was then living on the lot and may have built the present house. When in 1750 Thomas Dickinson inherited a houselot in Deerfield, John Dickinson (1707-1799) succeeded his brother as owner of the Hatfield property. This John Dickinson seems the more likely builder of the house and was probably responsible for the doorway, possibly after the death of his father in 1762.   *Illustrated*

Features: vine-carved pilasters, foliage pilaster caps, thumbprint decoration on keystone, doubled outline, double doors.

[134]   Carved pilaster capital. Doorway of the John Dickinson house. (photograph 1983)

[134] Doorway of the John Dickinson house, Hatfield, Massachusetts, constructed ca. 1762. (photograph 1934)

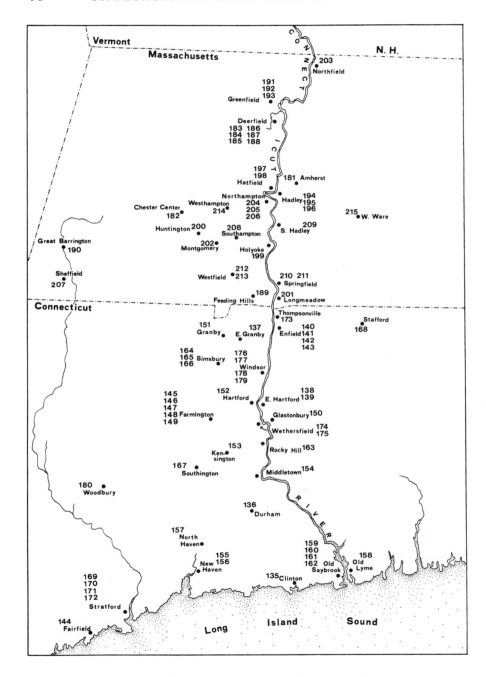

Figure 6   Distribution of flat-top doorways in the Connecticut River Valley.

Flat-Top Doorways

Connecticut

135. Clinton: House of Adam Stanton (ca. 1748-1834).**

In 1791 Adam Stanton, who moved to Clinton (then Killingworth) from Rhode Island, purchased and completed the house begun in 1789 by Capt. Walter Hilliard and his brothers. In 1916 his grandson Lewis Eliot Stanton created the John A. Stanton Memorial in honor of his brother. A museum of early American furnishings, the house is owned by the Hartford National Bank and Trust Company. A flat-top doorway is visible under a front portico (Colonial Dames; *Stanton House*).

Features: panels at termination of pilasters, no moldings between panels and fluting, eight-petal rosettes in pilaster caps, pulvinated frieze but no cornice, double doors with X panels.

136. Durham: unknown house.

A doorway from Durham was sold by Myra Linton, a dealer, to Albro Case, a builder, who moved it to the Elijah Mather house at 256 Palisado Avenue, Windsor, Connecticut, about 1963.

Features: pedestals restored, six-petal rosettes in pilaster caps, duck-bill keystone, cornice probably a restoration, double doors.

137. East Granby: House of Luke Thrall (1753-1829).**†

Land and probate records fail to indicate the date of this house. It may have been built about 1780, the year that Luke Thrall married; or it may have been built earlier by John Thrall, the father of Luke Thrall, and have been given to Luke at the time of his marriage. The style of the doorway corresponds with the 1780 date. The house is also known as the Nicholson house, the Nicholsons being later owners. *Illustrated*

Features: fans below fluting on pilasters, two vertical lozenge-shaped tablets in each pilaster cap, truncated keystone, entablature compressed and above an overhang, single door, width sufficient for former double doors.

138. East Hartford: "Comstock" House.*

Charles Woolsey Lyon purchased a flat-top doorway about 1920-1925 from a contractor who had recently torn down a house in East Hartford (Charles Woolsey Lyon to AFM, 1959). Lyon eventually placed it on the front entrance of The

Silver Horn, a restaurant in Millbrook, New York. He referred to the doorway as coming from the "Comstock" house. Land records indicate that on 9 June 1857 William G. Comstock purchased twenty-one acres with buildings in East Hartford from Henry Olmsted who had moved to Iowa. But apparently the house on the Henry Olmsted place burned in 1875 and Comstock built "an elegant mansion, the best residence in the town" (*Hartford County Biographies*, p. 761). Although efforts to obtain a complete history of the Comstock house have been unsuccessful, the following paragraph written in 1879 by the Reverend Joseph O. Goodwin, historian of East Hartford, suggests that Comstock moved the house he bought from Olmsted and built a new house in 1857. It was probably the 1857 house that burned.

> Col. George Pitkin lived in the Jas. Root house, now Comstock's . . . Col. William Pitkin (4th) lived on the site now occupied by Mr. Wm. G. Comstock. His house is still standing, having been moved down on "Pondrette Lane," on the J.C. Bull Place. (*East Hartford History*, p. 213).

The doorway may have had a pediment at one time.

Features: six-petal rosettes in pilaster caps, fluted keystone, doubled outline, double doors.

139.   East Hartford: House of Elisha Pitkin (1733-1819).**†

According to land records of 1758, Elisha Pitkin received property without a house from his father Col. Joseph Pitkin. Another deed of 1760 described the lot as the place where Elisha Pitkin "now lives." The large gambrel-roofed house that was moved to North Guilford in the 1950s was apparently built 1758-1760.

Features: six-petal rosettes in pilaster caps, keystone rounded on end, doubled outline, double doors with X panels.

140.   Enfield: House of Dr. Simeon Field (1731-1801).**

Standing on the west side of the main street, this house has a marker with the date 1763. The modest doorway probably never had a pediment.

Features: undecorated pilaster caps and keystone, sufficient width for former double doors.

141.   Enfield: House of Ephraim Pease (1719-1801).**

The date of this house on the main street is uncertain. There is an overhang, apparently hewn, to which a triangular pediment has been adapted on the side door. A pediment on the front door may have been removed when a nineteenth-century porch was added. Pilaster caps, keystone, and the entire entablature are also missing.

Features: (remaining) panelled pedestals, fat moldings, fluted pilasters, rusticated surround, single door.

142. Enfield: House of the Reverend Elam Potter (1742-1794).**

This house, greatly altered, stands just south of the Ephraim Pease house (141) and has a marker with the date 1769, which was the year Elam Potter was installed at Enfield and the year that he married Sybil Pease, daughter of Ephraim Pease. A flat-top side door has a cornice above an overhang, an architrave and frieze below. A twentieth-century front porch conceals any traces of a possible former pediment. The eighteenth-century interior trim is elaborate.

Features: undecorated pilaster caps and keystone, single door.

143. Enfield: unknown house.

A heavy flat-top doorway known from a 1930s photograph and said to be in Enfield (Chamberlain, *Doorways*, p. 19) has not been located.

Features: (from photograph) wide pilasters with twelve(?) flutes, undecorated pilaster caps and keystone, double doors with X panels.

144. Fairfield: House of Samuel Penfield (1734-1811).**

Said to have been built immediately after the Revolution (Trowbridge, p. 391), this house has been greatly altered. If the doorway ever had a pediment, it was removed when a porch was built across the front of the house. The house is commonly known as the Sun Tavern.

Features: rectangular panelled pedestals cut off at bottom for floor of porch, fluted keystone, entablature missing because of porch.

145. Farmington: House of Lt. Solomon Cowles (1719-1793).**

Research by the Farmington historian Mabel Spencer Hurlburt indicates that the front of this house at 149 Main Street was built by Judah Woodruff for Solomon Cowles in 1765 (Farmington Catalogue) as an addition to an earlier house once owned by Isaac Cowles. In 1765 the early house was made into an ell of the new house. The flat-top doorway adapted to a front overhang reaches nearly to the window above offering insufficient space for a pediment.

Features: pilaster caps missing, architrave including keystone decorated with dentil-like course, double doors.

146. Farmington: House of Col. Fisher Gay (1733-1776).

The accounts of Fisher Gay indicate that this house was built in 1766 and 1767 and that Judah Woodruff among others worked on it. In 1901 the house, then the Farmington Country Club, burned. The doorway is known from an early photograph (*Farmington Homes*).

Features: (from photograph) double doors.

147. Farmington: House of John Hart (1686-1753).**

The date of about 1745 assigned to this house (Colonial Dames) cannot be verified. An early photograph (SPNEA) indicates that the present beaded clapboards and double doors are restorations. The doorway, whose pilaster caps are nearly identical to those on the meeting house of 1771 built by Judah Woodruff, may have been commissioned by a later owner of the house than John Hart and may be the work of Judah Woodruff.   *Illustrated*

Features: pilaster caps contain two pairs of carved leaves under two-dimensional Ionic volutes; above the door the entablature (or pediment) has concave curves on each side and a keystone consisting of a foliage-carved panel.

148. Farmington: House of John Mix (1755-1834).**

The front part of this house, just south of the burying ground, is said to have been built in 1785 by Judah Woodruff for John Mix (Farmington Catalogue). A nineteenth-century porch at the front entrance, now taken off but known from an early photograph (*Farmington Homes*), may have caused the removal of a former pediment on this doorway whose entablature rises above a front overhang.

Features: no pilaster caps, architrave including keystone decorated with dentil-like course, single door.

149. Farmington: Third Meeting House.**

Raised in 1771 (Kelly, *Meetinghouses*, 1:161), this meeting house was designed by Judah Woodruff of Farmington. However, this attribution is derived from an address delivered by Noah Porter (1811-1892) in 1872 and not from surviving church records (CSL) whose only mention of Judah Woodruff in connection with the meeting house was on 6 February 1769 when he and Fisher Gay were chosen a committee "to Procure thick Stuff" for the proposed edifice. Three doorways on the meeting house, a main doorway covered by a later porch, which may once have had a pediment, and two flat-top side doorways, all have Ionic volutes on the pilaster caps similar to those on Judah Woodruff's own house in Farmington. In his address of 1872, Dr. Noah Porter, then president of Yale, referred to the pulpit carved by Woodruff with vines representing English ivy (*Historical Discourse*, in Kelly, *Meetinghouses*, 1:162). In 1834, according to church records, the congregation voted on repairs that included the removal of the pulpit and canopy, or sounding board, and the construction of a small portico over the front door.

Features: (on main doorway) pilaster caps contain two pairs of carved leaves under two-dimensional Ionic volutes, tapered keystone, double doors.

150. Glastonbury: House of Deacon Benjamin Talcott (1674-1727).

Labels on two drawings of this house made in 1828 by Laurilla A. Smith of Glastonbury (CHS), a front view and a view of the left side, state that the house was built in 1699 by Deacon Benjamin Talcott (who married that year), that it was razed in 1851, and that it was the home of the Reverend William Lockwood from 1797 to 1828. The drawings show a flat-top doorway on the front of the house and a triangular pediment on the side door. These doorways must have been added to the house by a later owner if indeed the house was built in 1699.

151. Granby: House of Judah Holcomb (ca. 1705-1802). **†

Until 1786 the town of Granby, originally called Salmon Brook, was a part of Simsbury. According to land records of 1747, Judah Holcomb purchased 78¾ acres of land at Salmon Brook parish from John Saxton, it being the land "on which the said Judah Holcomb's now dwelling house Standeth." The doorway, which probably never had a pediment, is of a style associated with the 1770s and may date to the marriage of Judah Holcomb, Jr., in 1774. It is also possible that the present gambrel-roofed house is later than the one referred to in 1747.

Features: pedestals missing, foliage pilaster caps, thumbprint keystone, single door, width sufficient for former double doors.

[147]   Doorway of the John Hart house, Farmington, Connecticut, possibly constructed about 1770 for an earlier house. (photograph ca. 1920s)

Greenwich: House of Gale Carter, see West Ware, Massachusetts: unknown house (215).

Haddam: House of the Reverend Phineas Fiske, see Montgomery, Massachusetts: unknown house (202).

152. Hartford: House of Col. Samuel Talcott (bp. 1711-1797).

An early photograph (CHS) identified as "Talcott or Wainwright House, Main Street, Hartford" shows a center-chimney house with a pitched roof, a double overhang, and a flat-top doorway under the front overhang. This house, according to William L. Warren (Warren, *Talcott*), was built in 1770 by Samuel Talcott, son of Gov. Joseph Talcott. The last member of the Talcott family to occupy the house was a daughter of Thomas G. Talcott who married W.A.M. Wainwright. The house was torn down in 1910.

Features: (from photograph) high panelled pedestals, fat moldings above pedestals, decorative work on cornice, double doors with X panels.

153. Kensington: House of the Reverend William Burnham (ca. 1684-1750).

A Whitefield drawing of a house (SPNEA) is labelled "Built probably by Rev. Mr. Burnham, the first minister settled here. It has been moved." No details of a doorway are discernible in the drawing; however, a later photograph entitled "The Home of Rev. William Burnham 1709" shows a flat-top doorway adapted to a front overhang. The town agreed to build a house for the minister as part of his settlement in 1709, which, according to specifications in town records, had only two rooms on the ground floor and was considerably smaller than the two-chimney, center-hall house of the photograph (*Kensington Church*, facing p. 30, p. 34). Either the 1709 house was at some point extensively enlarged and the doorway added during alterations or it was pulled down and a new house built, which seems a more likely possibility.

154. Middletown: House of Seth Wetmore (1700-1778).**

This house is said to have been built in 1746, the year of Seth Wetmore's marriage. On the basis of disturbed clapboards over the front door, a descendant of Seth Wetmore added a scroll pediment to an existing flat-top doorway about 1923 according to Samuel Green, the current owner. Samuel Green also stated in 1970 that when the house was remodelled in either 1917 or 1923 a gambrel roof was removed as was a side doorway; fragments of its pilasters survive in his cellar. The house has triangular window pediments.

Features: fluted pedestals, six-petal rosettes in pilaster caps, duck-bill keystone, doubled outline, rusticated surround, width sufficient for former double doors.

155. New Haven: House on Church Street.

An early nineteenth-century watercolor (NHCHS), primarily illustrating the First Episcopal Church (17), shows the southeast corner of Church and Chapel streets in 1790 and suggests that the house just to the right or south of the church had a flat-top doorway.

156. New Haven: House at corner of Church and Chapel streets.

The watercolor depicting the First Episcopal Church (17;155) suggests that the house on the corner of Church and Chapel streets had a flat-top doorway.

157. North Haven: House of Gideon Todd, Jr. (ca. 1738-1817).**

Although an old tavern sign for this house, also known as the Rising Sun Tavern, is said to have had the date 1738 on it (Colonial Dames), the style of the present house suggests that it was built about 1771, the year Gideon Todd, Jr., was first licensed as a tavern keeper. It may have replaced an earlier house of 1738. The house stands on Old Tavern Road.

Features: undecorated pilaster caps, double doors.

158. Old Lyme: House of Samuel Mather (1745-1809).**

Built about 1770 (Kelly, *Houses*, p. 84), this house later became a parsonage. The tall doorway reaching nearly to the window above could never have had a pediment. The doorway bears a strong resemblance to the doorways on the Nathaniel Jones, Jr., house (159) and the Capt. Stephen Riley house (163).

Features: tall pilasters on short pedestals, multiple fine fluting in pilaster caps, double doors (not original).

159. Old Saybrook: House of Nathaniel Jones, Jr. (bp. 1744). †

This house, formerly at 163 Main Street, was taken down in 1976 and stored by the 18th Century Company of Durham. Land records indicate that Nathaniel Jones, Jr., who married in 1768, sold his homelot "with a new dwelling house thereon" to William Hart, Jr., in 1772. In 1783 Hart sold it to Dr. Elisha Ely (1748-1801) by whose name the house is locally known. The house stood just north of the Samuel Willard house (162), also with a flat-top doorway. The doorway bears a strong resemblance to the doorways on the Samuel Mather house (158) and on the Capt. Stephen Riley house (163).

Features: tall unfluted pilasters with short pedestals, undecorated pilaster caps, no surround, single door.

[163]   Doorway of the Capt. Stephen Riley house, Rocky Hill, Connecticut, built ca. 1764. (photograph 1983)

160. Old Saybrook: House of Capt. Willoughby Lynde (1761-1817).**

A modest flat-top doorway was constructed to fit under a front overhang on this gambrel-roofed house at 174 North Cove Road. A marker on the house gives its traditional 1799 date.

Features: undecorated pilaster caps, single door.

161. Old Saybrook: House of William Tully (1709-1775).**

This house at 135 North Cove Road is dated 1750 on the reverse of an old photograph (CHS), probably on the basis that William Tully married his second wife Elizabeth Lay of Lyme in that year. The top of the doorway reaches to the window above.

Features: tall unfluted pilasters on short pedestals, twelve-petal rosettes in pilaster caps, keystone cut off, doubled outline, sufficient width for former double doors.

162. Old Saybrook: House of Samuel Willard (1715-1786). †

In 1740 according to land records, the Reverend William Hart (1713-1784), who was ordained in 1736, purchased a home on this lot from Samuel Willard. However, the house with flat-top doorway, known from a photograph of about 1885 (CHS) that is identified as the Hart house on Main Street, was probably improved by Elisha Hart (ca. 1785-1842), son of the minister. Elisha Hart was married in 1780 and inherited the property from his father.

Features: (from photograph) double doors.

163. Rocky Hill: House of Capt. Stephen Riley (1732-1813).**

Records at the Rocky Hill Historical Society give 1742-1745 for the construction of this house at 660 Old Main Street and further state that Stephen Riley (1698-1755) built it for his son Stephen Riley, Jr. (1732-1813). The architectural historian Elmer Davenport Keith assigned it a date of 1770-1780 (E.D. Keith to AFM 5 April 1960). The tall flat-top doorway that reaches nearly to the window above could not ever have had a pediment but does seem related to the later period. Capt. Stephen Riley, who was married about 1764, may have kept tavern in the house that has been called "Old Tavern — Rocky Hill" (Kelly, *Houses*, pl. 22). The doorway bears a resemblance to those on the Nathaniel Jones, Jr., house (159) and the Samuel Mather house (158).   *Illustrated*

Features: undecorated pilaster caps, no keystone, double doors.

164. Simsbury (Weatogue): House of Jonathan Humphrey (b. 1688).**

A marker on this house gives the date 1720, which if correct means that the doorway was added at a much later period, possibly just before or just after the Revolution. While clearly of the Connecticut River Valley style (with among other features a pulvinated frieze and rosettes), the treatment is light and lacking in boldness. The top of the doorway is flush with the window above. The doorway is an almost exact duplicate of the doorway on the nearby William Wilcockson, Jr., house (166).

Features: eight-petal double rosettes in pilaster caps, dentil and modillion courses in cornice, truncated keystone, double doors with X panels.

165. Simsbury: House of Capt. Elisha Phelps (1737-1776).**

A marker on this house gives the date 1771. The doorway probably once had a pediment.

Features: base and pedestals restored, foliage pilaster caps, entablature missing, double doors.

166. Simsbury (Weatogue): House of William Wilcockson, Jr. (1702-1772).**

A marker on this house gives the date 1723, the year when William Wilcockson, Jr., married "Thanks" Adams. If this date is correct, the doorway was added at a much later period. The doorway is an almost exact duplicate of the doorway on the nearby Jonathan Humphrey house (164).

Features: delicate foliage carving on pedestals, eight-petal double rosettes on pilaster caps, dentils and modillions in cornice, pointed keystone, double doors (not original).

167. Southington: House of Job Lewis (1731-1813).**

This house, more commonly called the Sally Lewis (bp. 1773-1840) house after his daughter, was built by Job Lewis probably about the time of his marriage in 1755. The doorway, adapted to a front overhang, may have been added to the house at a later time. Its appearance suggests a 1780s date.

Features: two vertical lozenge-shaped tablets in each pilaster cap, truncated keystone, compressed entablature adapted to a front overhang, double doors.

168. Stafford: House of the Reverend John Willard (1733-1807).**

This house stands facing the town common on the old road from Hartford to Worcester. The doorway that almost reaches the window above could never have had a pediment. The Reverend John Willard was ordained at Stafford in

1757, but the doorway and perhaps also the house appear to be later.
Features: fans below fluting on pilasters, two vertical lozenge-shaped tablets in each pilaster cap, truncated keystone, frieze and cornice missing, double doors.

Illustrated

[168]   Doorway of the Reverend John Willard house, Stafford, Connecticut.

169. Stratford: House of Henry Curtis, Jr. (1751-1814).**

This house at 2134 Elm Street is said to have been built in 1788 (Wilcoxson, p. 424) but appears to be earlier. A flat-top doorway that may have had a pediment survives under a porch. Henry Curtis, Jr., married Phebe Sherman in 1778.

Features: six-petal rosettes in pilaster caps, tapered keystone, frieze and cornice missing, double doors.

170. Stratford: House of Stephan Frost (b. 1747).**

This house at 2302 Elm Street is said to have been built in 1769 (Wilcoxson, p. 292) by Stephan Frost who married in 1772.

Features: tall fluted pilasters with short pedestals, undecorated pilaster caps, diminutive keystone, single door.

171. Stratford: House of Lt. William Thompson (1742-1777).**

Located at 904 East Broadway, this house is dated 1761 by a marker, the date probably being based on the marriage of William Thompson in 1760. The doorway may have had a pediment before a front porch was added.

Features: tall fluted pilasters with bases destroyed, undecorated pilaster caps, no keystone, width sufficient for former double doors.

172. Stratford: 1598 Main Street.**

Efforts to trace the history of the house at 1598 Main Street have not been entirely successful. The flat-top doorway is obscured by a late-nineteenth-century porch, and double doors of the same period have round-headed glass panels. The house sits on a late brick foundation that suggests that it may have been moved, a probability consistent with findings of Raymond D. Cable of nearby Devon, who reports that the 1868 Beers Atlas shows a schoolhouse on this corner (Beers Atlas, *New Haven County*). According to Mr. Cable, most of Stratford's one-room schools were replaced when a new and large school was opened on East Broadway in 1885. An 1884 map of Stratford shows a house on this southeast corner of Main Street and South Avenue owned by C. Burrett, presumably the present structure, moved onto the lot vacated after 1868 by the school. The original location and owner of the house, however, have not been determined.

Features: tall fluted pilasters on short pedestals, six-petal rosettes on pilaster caps, diminutive keystone, a band of narrow dentils across frieze, double doors (not original).

173. Thompsonville: unknown house.

H.A. Armstrong of New Haven reported to William L. Warren in 1959 that a house with a flat-top doorway was taken down the previous year in Thompsonville and that he believed the doorway was saved.

174. Wethersfield: House of Silas Deane (1737-1789).**

In 1765 Silas Deane purchased the land on which he built his house (*Wethersfield History*, 1:481) with a flat-top doorway. The doorway never had a pediment. However, after the removal of a Victorian porch from the front of the house in the 1940s (whose construction might have sealed the fate of a pediment), evidence of a porch that was apparently an original feature of the house was uncovered in the early 1960s. During extensive restoration work, a set of mortises was found on the front second-story plate that was earlier than the Victorian mortises. These early mortises may have been cut when the house was originally framed in order to hold rafters for the roof of a porch. Further evidence of such a porch as an original feature lies in the foundation work of the house. Across the front where a porch would obscure it from view, the masonry is of undressed stone, while on each side the stone is ashlar.

That Silas Deane would choose to have a doorway of the Connecticut River Valley style at his front entrance, albeit in the shadow of a porch or piazza, stresses the regard for these doorways held by substantial or would-be prominent members of a community. Deane commissioned an asymetrical house with an innovative floor plan, but he did not reject the doorway symbolic of wealth and importance.

A glass plate negative of the house with the original porch is at the Wethersfield Historical Society.

Features: undecorated pedestals, pilaster caps and keystone, no pulvinated frieze, heavy modillions in cornice, doubled outline, wide single door with X panels.

175. Wethersfield: House of Ezekiel Williams (1729-1818).**

In 1759, a year prior to his marriage, Ezekiel Williams purchased land from the town (*Wethersfield History*, 2:815) and probably then began to build his house. Although features remaining on the doorway suggest that it once had a scroll pediment, perhaps removed in the 1930s when, according to John C. Willard of Wethersfield, an unsightly two-story porch was placed across the facade, a Whitefield drawing (SPNEA) shows the doorway as a flat-top. If there was once a pediment, it had disappeared by the 1880s.

Features: moldings above and below fluting on pilasters missing but outlined in paint, six-petal rosettes in pilaster caps, keystone missing, frieze and cornice cut off for porch, rusticated surround, width sufficient for former double doors.

176. Windsor: House of Alexander Allyn (1718-1790).**

More generally known as the Fyler house and dated 1640 or 1645 in a report of 1925 when it was acquired by the Windsor Historical Society, the house was actually built after 1763 by Alexander Allyn when he purchased an unimproved parcel of the Fyler homelot according to recent research by William L. Warren. The doorway, now covered by a porch, may have had a pediment before the porch was added.

Features: pedestals cut off for porch floor, seven-petal rosettes in pilaster caps, no keystone, top of cornice cut off, single door with X panel.

[180]   Doorway of the John Orton house (Orton Tavern), Woodbury, Connecticut, probably built about 1763. (photograph ca. 1920s)

177. Windsor: House of Jonathan Ellsworth (1716-1775), altered.**

A photograph published in 1913 (*Reclaiming the Old House*, facing p. 27), of a house with a flat-top doorway adapted to a front overhang and labelled "One of the Ellsworth houses at Windsor, Vt." is now known to show the house of Jonathan Ellsworth at 273 Palisado Avenue, Windsor, Connecticut, also called the Alexander Ellsworth house for Jonathan's son who inherited the property. Since the photograph was taken, a portico has been placed at the front entrance; but elements of the former doorway remain.

Features: pedestals and pilasters remain in place, cornice and keystone on gable of the portico.

178. Windsor: House of Jonathan Ellsworth, Jr. (1743-1806).

An early photograph of a house (WiHS) identified as the "Jonathan Ellsworth house, 1784, Palisado Ave. Windsor, Conn." shows a hipped-roof house with a flat-top doorway. The doorway has since disappeared; this house at 336 Palisado Avenue now has a reproduction scroll doorway dating to a restoration of the 1960s.

Features: (from photograph) high pedestals, fat moldings, rosettes in pilaster caps, single door, sufficient width for former double doors.

179. Windsor: House of the Reverend William Russell (1725-1775).**

In 1754 the Reverend William Russell was ordained in Windsor, and the house and doorway were probably constructed in that year. The doorway may have had a scroll pediment.

Features: eight-petal rosettes in pilaster caps, duck-bill keystone, rusticated surround, double doors (not original).

180. Woodbury: House of John Orton (1692-1778).

John Orton moved to Woodbury from Farmington about 1717 and according to local histories built this house about 1730. Land records indicate that he deeded his house to his son John Orton, Jr. (1729-1818), in 1763 shortly before John Jr.'s marriage that year. John Orton, Jr., probably added the doorway, and he may have built an entirely new house. The house of John Orton, known as the Orton Tavern, remained in the Orton family until 1888. In 1922 it was sold to an actress, Miss M.L. Munn who, intending to move it to Great Neck, Long Island, had it taken down by the Whitney Co., 101 Park Avenue, New York. It was in storage in Bridgeport, Connecticut, when Miss Munn died soon after her purchase and has since disappeared (see *Woodbury Homes*, inside front cover). Efforts to trace the house have been unsuccessful. Early photographs (SPNEA) of the house show a doorway with unique features, slightly related to doorways in Farmington, Granby, and Southington.   *Illustrated*

Features: (from photographs) full-length pilasters with fluting on upper half only, pilaster caps carved with rows of small peaks or flames, duck-bill keystone, wide single door.

Massachusetts

181. Amherst: House of Solomon Boltwood (1727-1777).**

Dated 1745 on a plaque, this house was moved to Amity Street from a site just west of Lincoln Avenue according to Mason Dickinson who owned it in 1960. If the doorway once had a pediment adapted to a shallow front overhang, it was removed when a porch was added at the front entrance.

Features: undecorated pilaster caps, fluted keystone, single door.

182. Chester Center: House of Dr. Anson Boies (ca. 1784-1820).**†

Local tradition holds that this house was built by the Reverend Aaron Bascom for his daughter Charlotte at the time of her marriage to Dr. Anson Boies in 1810; and land records support the late date for this house and modest doorway, stating that in 1809 Bascom sold an unimproved acre and six rods to his future son-in-law. The doorway is not typical of the Connecticut River Valley style but has certain related elements such as a wide pulvinated frieze and the spirit of individuality. With a date of 1809, this doorway is the latest known. Similarities to the doorway on the Perley Cook house (199) just over the boundary in Huntington are noticeable.

Features: full-length pilasters, undecorated pilaster caps and keystone, doubled outline, single door.

Deerfield: Architectural Barn, see Hatfield: House of Richard Church (196).

183. Deerfield: House of Salah Barnard (1725-1795).**†

The north part of the house known as Frary house was probably built by Salah Barnard in 1765 at which time he sold old window frames, probably from an earlier house that belonged to the Frary family. In 1765 he paid for labor and building materials. Slightly prior to his death, Salah Barnard built an addition to the house on the south side with a flat-top doorway at the south entrance. This addition was called the "new house" when it was granted to Erastus Barnard (b. 1768) in the division of his father's estate in 1796. Erastus Barnard operated a tavern in his house from 1796 to 1804, sold it to H.W. Strong in 1805, and moved to Canandaigua, New York. In 1890 C. Alice Baker purchased both the north and south parts of the house, which she restored. Long open to the public, the house has been owned by Historic Deerfield, Inc., since 1969. The motif of the flat-top doorway was copied in the 1950s on a reproduction triangular pedimented doorway on the front of the house.

Features: full-length fluted pilasters, undecorated pilaster caps, no keystone, frieze decorated with interlocking applied circles and with dentils, modillions in cornice, single door.

184. Deerfield: House of Eliezer Hawks (1693-1774).**

Now a two-story ell of an early-nineteenth-century house, the eighteenth-century house of Eliezer Hawks faces south on the east side of the street in the settlement of Wapping a few miles south of the Deerfield street. The doorway may relate to about 1765, the year of the marriage of Paul Hawks, son of Eliezer, although the eighteenth-century house appears to have been constructed earlier.

Features: six-petal rosettes in pilaster caps, fluted keystone, rusticated surround, double doors (not original).

185. Deerfield: House of Jeremiah Nims (1721-1797).**†

Possibly built by John Nims (1679-1762), father of Jeremiah, this house originally had a pitched roof and faced south. According to local tradition, the house was built in 1710 and took its present form, that of a gambrel-roofed house facing west, three-quarters of a century later (Sheldon, 1:618). This major alteration, of which there is evidence in the location of the stairway at the south door, may have been accomplished in 1786 when Jeremiah Nims made out his will in favor of his son Seth Nims (1762-1831) or about 1783 when Seth Nims married. The doorway standing on the south side of the house (original front) is closely related to the south door of Salah Barnard's house next north (183).

Features: undecorated pedestals, undecorated pilaster caps, no keystone, pulvinated frieze on pilasters only, dentil course on cornice, single door.

Deerfield: North Meadows (Dray house), see Greenfield: House of Abner Wells (192).

186. Deerfield: House of David Sexton (1734-1800).**†

At a town meeting on 17 April 1761, it was voted to sell thirty rods of the Deerfield street or common to David Sexton. On this lot Sexton soon began to build a house. From March through July 1762 his brother-in-law, Joseph Barnard, charged him for carting stone, slitwork, boards, brick, glass, and lath. On 31 July Joseph Barnard recorded, ''Br Sexton Dr to myself 1½ Days to Lath your House'' (Barnard, Joseph account books). During the Revolution David Sexton operated a tavern in his house. Nineteenth-century photographs (PVMA library) show a porch over the front door that has since been removed. The present flat-top doorway, probably constructed in 1762, may have had a pediment prior to the period of the porch.

Features: pedestals restored, six-petal rosettes in pilaster caps, duck-bill keystones, double doors (not original).

187. Deerfield: unidentified.*

In 1968 a flat-top doorway with no identification was discovered in a shed on the north side of the Joseph Stebbins house in Deerfield. It may have come from a Deerfield house, or it may have been purchased by Mr. and Mrs. Henry N. Flynt and stored for some future restoration, although in 1968 neither could remember it. The doorway, painted gray-green, was placed in the PVMA museum.

Features: pedestals missing, seven-petal rosettes in pilaster caps, undecorated keystone, width sufficient for former double doors.

188. Deerfield: unlocated.

A photograph found in 1968 in the files of Historic Deerfield, Inc. (then The Heritage Foundation), shows an unidentified flat-top doorway. The photograph had been previously labelled "In D B Storage" (Dwight Barnard House, Deerfield, a property of Historic Deerfield, Inc.). The doorway was probably purchased by Mr. and Mrs. Henry N. Flynt from William E. Gass of South Deerfield. In 1968 the doorway could not be located and has not as yet been found.

[191] Amos Allen house, Greenfield, Massachusetts, built ca. 1766. (photograph 1890s)

Features: (from photograph) undecorated pedestals (possibly replacements), six-petal rosettes in pilaster caps, duck-bill keystone, double doors (not original).

189. Feeding Hills: House of Abraham Burbank, Jr. (1739-1808).**†

In 1764 Abraham Burbank, Jr., of Suffield, Connecticut, purchased land and buildings from Benjamin Leonard, Jr., of Springfield for £ 390. The deed stated that the land was on both sides of the road leading from Westfield to Suffield and was sold "together with barn Edifices and buildings thereon." In spite of the relatively large price for that time, the present house does not appear to have been included in the sale and was probably built by Burbank. In 1958 a nineteenth-century porch stood across the entire front of the house. This was removed between 1961 and 1963. As only a space of fifteen inches exists between the top of the doorway and the window above, the possibility of a former pediment is remote.

Illustrated

Features: eight-petal rosettes in pilaster caps, twelve-petal oval rosette in keystone, width sufficient for former double doors.

190. Great Barrington: House of Gen. Joseph Dwight (1703-1765).**

Local history holds that Joseph Dwight and his second wife Abigail Williams, the widow of the Reverend John Sergeant of Stockbridge, resided in Stockbridge until about 1757, that they purchased land in Great Barrington in 1759, and that they soon built a house (*Great Barrington History*, p. 176). Beginning in 1759 through 1763, Dwight owed small sums to Elijah Williams of Stockbridge that were related to construction. On 16 April 1761 Dwight was charged for a mason and mason tender who worked eleven and a half days "building the Kitchen Chimney" (Williams, Ephraim and Elijah account book). Moved from its original site to a lot behind the former Berkshire Inn, the house had a front porch in the 1920s. Before the porch there may have been a pediment. The house has a triangular pediment over the side door stylistically related to a front triangular doorway in neighboring Sheffield (123).

Features: undecorated pilaster caps, duck-bill keystone, double doors.

191. Greenfield: House of Amos Allen (1722-1797).**

Amos Allen moved from Deerfield to Greenfield and built a house in the Greenfield meadows in 1766. There he kept tavern and was first licensed in 1768 (*Greenfield History*, pp. 605, 795). Although a porch stood across the front of the house in this century (as evidenced by outlines in paint after the porch was removed), a nineteenth-century photograph (privately owned, copy AFM) taken prior to the addition of the porch shows the doorway with no pediment. If there was at one time a pediment, it had disappeared before the porch was added.

Illustrated

Features: six-petal rosettes in pilaster caps with small circular indented centers, keystone perhaps cut off, doubled outline, double doors.

192. Greenfield: House of Abner Wells (1742-1835.)*†

In 1968 an eighteenth-century house belonging to Thomas W. Merrigan was torn down at 53 Congress Street, a street that was opened in 1852 through unimproved land purchased by Henry W. Clapp in 1843. A title search indicated that the early house was moved from a lot at the east end of Main Street that Clapp had bought in 1835 to Congress Street before 1858 when it appears on a wall map as "HW Clapp" (*Franklin County Map*). The lot was the former homelot of Abner Wells. In 1785 Abner Wells purchased his brother Joel's interest in the homelot of their father, Joshua Wells. Abner Wells probably tore down the house of Joshua Wells and built a new one shortly after 1785. Architecturally the house and doorway formerly at 53 Congress Street agree with a date of 1785. In 1969 the doorway became the property of Alfred J. Dray, who had it placed on his newly built house in the north meadows in Deerfield.
Features: short pedestals, tall fluted pilasters, undecorated pilaster caps, single door.

193. Greenfield: House of Capt. Ebenezer Wells (1723-1787).*

In the 1930s a flat-top doorway, said to have stood on the house of Ebenezer Wells (a brother of the above Abner Wells) in the Greenfield meadows, was sold by Macy's Department Store to Ralph Carpenter who placed it on his house at 55 Morris Street, Scarsdale, New York. In 1968 Mr. Carpenter stated that he did not know how long the doorway had been in the possession of the store.
Features: eight-petal rosettes in pilaster caps, fluted keystone, doubled outline, rusticated surround, double doors.

194. Hadley: House of Dr. William Porter (1763-1847).**†

In 1762 according to land records, Eleazer Porter, father of William Porter, purchased two acres of land adjoining the north side of his homelot that descended to William Porter in a division of his father's estate in 1798. The house was built by William Porter in 1789 according to Sylvester Judd (Judd ms.), the year after William Porter's marriage. That it belonged to William Porter and not to his father is made clear in Eleazer Porter's will of 1797, which left his wife one-third of all the buildings on his homelot "Except those Buildings called William Porter's." The doorway, generally massive and heavy, never had a pediment.
Features: ten flutes in pilasters, undecorated pilaster caps, five flutes in keystone, dentil course in cornice, modillions on cornice (now missing), double doors.

195. Hadley: House of Noah Smith (1707-1767).**†

Noah Smith owned this lot from 1724 until his death in 1767 and probably built the house, but it may have been built by his son Warham Smith (1735-1802) who inherited the property. In the nineteenth century when a porch was built across the front of the house, the frieze, cornice, and probably a scroll pediment were removed. The doorway has foliage carving associated with scroll pediments in Hadley, Hatfield, and Stockbridge. The porch was removed in the 1970s.

Features: foliage pilaster caps, decorated keystone, doubled outline, width sufficient for former double doors.

196. Hadley: House of Noah Smith, Jr. (b. 1732). †

When this house burned in April 1898 (unidentified clipping on reverse of a photograph of the house, FoL), it was known as the birthplace of Gen. Joseph Hooker (1814-1879). The nineteenth-century photograph shows a center-chimney, gambrel-roofed house, which was claimed in the clipping to have been built before 1700, with five windows on the facade. Standing on the west side of West Street slightly to the north of the road to the burying ground, the house occupied the north half of the original Richard Church homelot that was divided by the will of Samuel Church (1667-1694), who left the north half to his younger children. The house may have been built by John Church (b. 1692), son of Samuel, and enlarged to its gambrel form by Noah Smith, Jr., to whom John Church sold a four-acre lot with buildings in 1759 for £ 120. However, Noah Smith, Jr., probably pulled down the old house that he purchased and rebuilt shortly after 1759. When he sold the house to his brother Warham Smith in 1784, he received £ 751 for the property.

197. Hatfield: House of Richard Church (1675-1763). * †

In the 1950s William E. Gass of South Deerfield took down a house that stood on the south side of Elm Street west of the Mill River bridge. Photographs (HD) of this house, taken as the house was being dismantled, are labelled Edward Church house and show a center-chimney, five windows on the facade, and a partially enclosed porch at the front entrance. Edward Church (ca. 1628-1704), who left his homelot to his son Richard, may possibly have built the house toward the end of his life, but Richard Church seems the more likely candidate. Richard's sons John and Samuel, who inherited their father's homelot, probably added the doorway that is of a late period. Mr. and Mrs. Henry N. Flynt purchased what remained of the doorway, damaged by the Victorian porch, and stored it in Deerfield. Later it was placed on display in the Architectural Barn in Deerfield.

Features: pedestals missing, fans below fluting on pilasters, two vertical lozenge-shaped tablets in each pilaster cap, truncated or damaged keystone, architrave and frieze compressed, cornice replaced, single door.

198. Hatfield: House of James Porter (1714-1792). ** †

James Porter, who inherited the homelot of his father Ichabod Porter in 1727, probably built the house on the north side of Elm Street about the time of his marriage in 1737. The doorway is of a later period and, although simpler, resembles the doorway on the Richard Church house (196), especially in the area of the entablature. The house is located at 26 Elm Street.

Features: pedestals consist of a vertical board, no moldings, tall vertical undecorated pilaster caps, fluted keystone, entablature compressed, single door.

199. Holyoke: House of Lucas Morgan (bp. 1743-1818). †

About 1968 a house with a flat-top doorway standing at 1375 on the west side of Route 5 in Holyoke was moved to Virginia, but local residents could not give a more exact location. Called in 1891 the "Old Fairfield House" (*Picturesque Hampden*, p. 39), it was built by Lucas Morgan after 1774 when he received one hundred acres in the North Parish from the town of Springfield. In 1853 Roswell Morgan, son of Lucas, sold the house to Luther M. Fairfield. The doorway never had a pediment.

Features: full-length pilasters, eight-petal rosettes in pilaster caps, keystone abbreviated, entablature compressed, double doors.

200. Huntington: House of Perley Cook (d. 1854). ** †

In 1798 John Cook of Preston, Connecticut, sold ninety-five unimproved acres in Chester to his son Perley Cook who had married in 1795 and settled in Chester. When Perley Cook purchased two adjacent small parcels from Enoch Lee in 1807, the deed referred to Perley Cook's house. In 1853 a portion of the Cook property, including that on which the house stands, was annexed to Huntington (then Norwich) to the east. Located on Old State Road on the west corner of Chester Hill Road, the house, whose modest doorway appears similar to that on the nearby Dr. Anson Boies house (181) in Chester Center, faces the West Branch of the Westfield River.

Features: pedestals replaced, no fluting, undecorated pilaster caps and keystone, pulvinated frieze, single door.

201. Longmeadow: House of the Reverend Richard Salter Storrs (1763-1819). **

Headquarters of the Longmeadow Historical Society, this house is dated 1786, a date based on the marriage and the ordination of the Reverend Richard Salter Storrs in 1785. Annotations on a Whitefield drawing (SPNEA) state, "This house has been altered, how much I don't know. It has a piazza now." The doorway, which probably never had a pediment, is compatible with a date of 1786.

Features: undecorated pilaster caps, fluted keystone, double doors with X panels (may be replacements).

202. Montgomery: unknown house. *

A flat-top doorway was purchased by H.A. Armstrong of New Haven, Connecticut, from a house in Montgomery that was being wrecked. He sold it to Catharine (Brush) Ingham about 1954, and she placed it on the Reverend Phineas Fiske house in Haddam, Connecticut. The house, moved back from its original site, stands on the left of the road south of Haddam. The doorway closely resembles the one presently on the house (214) moved from West Ware, Massachusetts, to Greenwich, Connecticut.   *Illustrated*

Features: brickwork rustication in pedestals, undecorated pilaster caps, fluted keystone, entablature compressed, single door.

203. Northfield: House of Hezekiah Stratton, Jr. (1724-1800).**†

The date of this house of Hezekiah Stratton, who was a licensed tavern keeper prior to the Revolution, is uncertain, but it underwent several periods of construction. The front part of the house was probably built on 115½ acres of unimproved land deeded to Hezekiah Stratton by his brother Ebenezer Stratton in 1757, one year after the death of their father, Hezekiah Stratton, Sr. When Hezekiah Stratton, Jr., died in 1800, the property descended to his son, another Hezekiah (1766-1825), who added the ell on the west. In 1825 the probate court allotted to the third Hezekiah's widow "All west of the Kitchen in the new part of the deceaseds late dwelling house." In 1825 the farm consisted of 236 acres. While interior panelling in the front of the house is sophisticated, the doorway is modest and may well have been added as late as 1800 by the third Hezekiah.
Features: slender undecorated pedestals (perhaps replacements), slender pilasters, ruffled pilaster caps, fluted keystone (lower part missing), narrow pulvinated frieze, single door.

204. Northampton: House of Preserved Clapp (1675-1757).**†

When Ens. Josiah Clark purchased the homelot of Preserved Clapp on the northwest side of South Street in 1744, there was a house on the lot. A marker on the present house gives the date of 1704 but this cannot be verified. Josiah Clark, Jr., is reported to have lived on this homelot beginning in 1747 (*Northampton Graduates*, p. 180); but his full ownership began only in 1790 when he inherited it from his father. Josiah Clark, Jr.'s granddaughter married Hiram Ferry, and during the nineteenth century the house at the present 179 South Street became known as the Ferry house. The modest doorway adapted to a front overhang was probably added to the house in the 1770s.
Features: undecorated pedestals, no pilaster caps, entablature above overhang, single door.

205. Northampton: House of Samuel Edwards, Jr. (ca. 1676-1749).†

An early photograph (glass plate negative, FoL) labelled "Old House on site of Lathrop Home, Northampton, Mass." shows a house with a steeply pitched roof, center chimney, front and side overhangs, and what appears to be a flat-top doorway adapted to the overhang on the front entrance. Samuel Edwards, Jr., who originally owned this lot may have built the house in 1708 (*Northampton Graduates*, p. 112). His son Nathaniel Edwards (1729-1792) probably added the modest doorway. In 1868 Charles Edwards subdivided the property and probably tore down the old house. The house was gone by 1873 as indicated by a map of Northampton (Beers Atlas, *Hampshire County*) and was later replaced by the first Lathrop Home for Aged and Invalid Women that stood at 236 South Street on the south corner of Olive Street on property sold by Anna C. Edwards on 30 August 1887.

206. Northampton: House of Nathaniel Fowle (ca. 1750-1817). †

Standing at 139 Pleasant Street until the mid-1960s, this large gambrel-roofed house had an unsightly modern two-story porch across the front in 1959. A photograph taken by the Northampton architect Karl S. Putnam probably in the 1930s (now AFM) shows a sophisticated portico at the front entrance that appears to have replaced a pedimented doorway, elements of which survived until the house was torn down by the expanding Northampton Commercial College. Flanking the entrance were fluted pilasters whose pedestals were decorated with brickwork rustication. The surround was flaired at the top in the manner customary for pedimented doorways. Molded window cornices of an earlier period than the portico also support the probability of a pedimented doorway. A title search of the property indicated that the house was built after 1782 when Eliphaz Clapp, father-in-law of Nathaniel Fowle, deeded Fowle an unimproved acre of his own homelot and before 1785 when Clapp died and when Clapp's probate papers indicate that Fowle was established in an adjacent house.

Features: of remaining doorway elements (from photograph showing portico and from observations of AFM in 1959): brickwork pedestals, fluted pilasters, pilasters cut off a cornice probably when portico was built, flaired surround, width sufficient for former double doors.

207. Sheffield: House of Gen. John Ashley (1736-1799). **

Decorative elements such as foliage carved pilaster caps and pedestals with miniature scroll doorways relate the present flat-top doorway to the scroll pedimented doorways in South Windsor, Connecticut (29), and in Westfield, Massachusetts (63), and suggest that a scroll pediment was removed during nineteenth-century alterations, although no fragments of a scroll pediment remain. Included in these alterations was the addition of a front porch (now removed) seen in an early photograph (*Ashley Genealogy*, p. 97). The house and doorway may have been constructed about 1762 at the time of John Ashley's marriage. A side doorway, under a later porch, has foliage pilaster caps and may have had a triangular pediment.

Features: miniature scroll doorways on pedestals, foliage pilaster caps, keystone and part of architrave cut off when the doors were made higher, frieze and cornice removed for porch, doubled outline, rusticated surround, sufficient width for former double doors.

208. Southampton: unknown house. *

A simple flat-top doorway was found in a barn in Southampton about 1960 by Rudolph Hendrick and George Satler, who moved it to West Granville and placed it on a house behind the Curtis Tavern that they had previously moved from Maine. The doorway may have been a side doorway.

Features: horizontal incisions in pedestals, undecorated pilaster caps, no keystone, pulvinated frieze, single door.

209. South Hadley: House of Col. Benjamin Ruggles Woodbridge (1733-1819).**

Over the doors on this house are two dates, 1733 and 1787. The earlier date commemorates the first parsonage in South Hadley that became an ell of the present house (*South Hadley*, p. 96). The date 1787 represents the year Ruggles Woodbridge built his large center-chimney, gambrel-roofed house (*Hadley History*, p. 399 states "about 1788"). A 1920s photograph (SM) of the house shows the original double doors and is labelled Eastman house after owners in this century. The Skinner family of Holyoke used the house as a summer home early in this century. It is now the property of Mount Holyoke College.

Features: six-petal rosettes in pilaster caps, fluted keystone, double doors (original doors had S panels).

210. Springfield: Parsonage. †

In 1806 the Trustees of the Ministerial Fund sold the parsonage on the west side of Springfield's main street to Solomon Warriner for $2,850 with the provision that the minister, the Reverend Bezaliel Howard, could continue to use the premises for two more years. In 1819 Solomon Warriner sold his homestead to Daniel Bonticou. By 1879 the house had been moved to Hillman Street between Main and Dwight where it was used as a laundry and the Fallon Block occupied the Main Street site (*Connecticut Valley History*, 2:823). In 1890 the house was torn down (*Springfield Sketches*, p. 71). A photograph of a nineteenth-century engraving of the house (SPL), identified as the Daniel Bonticou house, shows a flat-top doorway. Although possibly earlier, the house was probably built about 1785 when the Reverend Bezaliel Howard was ordained.

Features: (from engraving) double doors.

211. Springfield: House of Zenas Parsons (1740-1818). †

According to land records, Zenas Parsons purchased a dwelling house and three acres of land from Luke and Jonathan Bliss in 1773, "being the Dwelling House and Homelot whereon the said Luke now Dwells." Court records indicate that Parsons was granted a tavern license that same year. A photograph published in 1893 of Parsons Tavern shows a three-story frame building with a flat-top main entrance and a side door with a triangular pediment (*Springfield Sketches*, p. 296). It seems possible that Parsons may have enlarged the house of Luke Bliss by raising the roof one story and that he also changed the location of the main entrance. Whereas the Luke Bliss house faced east onto Main Street, the ridge of the three-story house ran east to west; and the new facade opened onto Elm Street, then Meeting House Lane. Thus the doorway with the triangular pediment may have been the front entrance of the Luke Bliss house. In 1819, the year after Parsons's death, the tavern was moved from the southeast corner of Court Square to 72 West Court Street (ibid.) It has since been torn down.

Features: of flat-top doorway (from photograph) double doors with X panels.

212. Westfield: unknown house.*

A flat-top doorway was purchased about 1939 by owners of the Curtis Tavern, West Granville, and placed on the ell of the tavern. The sellers, Willard S. and Evelyn C. Fuller, stated that it came from a house in the Meadow Street section of Westfield that had been taken down.

Features: undecorated pilaster caps, fluted keystone, double doors.

213. Westfield: unknown house.

A flat-top doorway in Westfield is known from a drawing published in 1891 labelled "An Old Doorway" (*Picturesque Hampden*, p. 81).

Features: (from drawing) decorated pilaster caps, pulvinated frieze, rusticated surround.

West Granville: ell of Curtis Tavern, see Westfield: unknown house (212).

West Granville: on house behind Curtis Tavern, see Southampton: unknown house (208).

214. Westhampton: House of Jared Hunt (1760-1812).**†

Standing on a rise beyond the church in Westhampton is a center-chimney house with a modest front doorway with elements of the Connecticut River Valley style such as fluted pilasters and a pulvinated frieze. The house was probably built by Jared Hunt about the time of his marriage in 1783, while the property was awarded to him in a distribution of the estate of his father John Hunt (1712-1785). Described as "The Farm at Westhampton Containing one hundred & six acres," the land had previously been occupied by Abiathar French in 1773 (Judd ms.) and by Samuel Herring, both of whom lived in log houses (*Westhampton History*, p. 21).

Features: high pedestals (replaced), undecorated pilaster caps, no keystone, wide single door.

215. West Ware: unknown house with doorway from another unknown house.*

About 1934 William E. Gass of South Deerfield moved a house to Greenwich, Connecticut, for Gale Carter. The house, originally in West Ware, did not have a doorway; but Steve Racz of Milford, Connecticut, sold Gass a doorway for the house. Known from photographs taken of the house on its new site about 1935 (HD), the doorway, whose history is unknown, closely resembles the flat-top doorway formerly in Montgomery and moved to Haddam, Connecticut (201).

Features: (from photograph) brickwork rustication in pedestals, undecorated pilaster caps, fluted keystone, entablature compressed, double doors.

New Hampshire

216. Haverhill: House of Col. Charles Johnston.**

This house, located on the east side of Route 10, is dated 1770 on a nearby historic marker and 1769 on the house. The doorway has traces of the Connecticut River Valley style consisting of pilasters with pinched-in or mild hourglass-shaped pilaster caps. There may have been a pediment at one time.

217. Westmoreland: House of Maj. Isaac Butterfield (1742-1801).

A doorway, originally known from a photograph published in 1926 (White Pine 12, no. 5, p. 5) and clearly derived from those to the south in Massachusetts and Connecticut, was sold to Mrs. James Storrow about 1930 and was thought by residents of Westmoreland to be destined for Storrowtown in West Springfield, Massachusetts. Henry Ford was said to have been interested in the doorway also. Inquiries at Storrowtown and at The Henry Ford Museum have failed to locate the doorway. The house, known locally as the Evans Place, was still standing in the north part of town in 1959.

Features: (from photograph) full-length fluted pilasters, pilaster caps containing four double petals, shell-carved keystone, pulvinated frieze, single door.

New York

218. Brooklyn: unknown doorway.*

A flat-top doorway of unknown origin was purchased at an unrecorded date by the Brooklyn Museum from W. and J. Sloane. With fluted pilasters and a pulvinated frieze, this doorway probably came from the Connecticut River Valley.

Features: undecorated pedestals with guttae at top, undecorated pilaster caps, keystone not complete, dentil courses above and below cornice, single door.

Millbrook: Silver Horn, see East Hartford, Connecticut: "Comstock" House (138).

Scarsdale: 55 Morris Street, see Greenfield, Massachusetts: House of Capt. Ebenezer Wells (193).

Vermont

219. Bennington: House of Peter Harwood (1735-1815).

A Whitefield drawing of this house (Whitefield, *Vermont*) shows a flat-top doorway and has the following description: "This was built by Peter Harwood, one of the first settlers in Bennington, about 1772. It is in a good state of preservation and has a handsome front door. It stands near the foot of Mt. Anthony." Another source (*Bennington Sketches*, p. 32) gives the date 1769 for the house, a date apparently supplied in a diary kept by Benjamin Harwood, son of Peter. Although born at Concord, Massachusetts, Peter Harwood resided in Amherst prior to his settling in Bennington. The house was restored in 1909 by Seymour Van Santvoord (*Troy Times*, 28 September 1909) whose son, George Van Santvoord, reported that during the restoration original elements were disturbed and that the doorway did not survive. Early photographs of the house are in the files of the Bennington Museum, but details of the doorway are indistinct.

220. Chester: unidentified house.**

A doorway with elements of the Connecticut River Valley style stands on a house on Route 103 between Rockingham and Chester.

Features: undecorated pedestals, fluted pilasters, undecorated pilaster caps, pulvinated frieze, molded cornice, single door.

Appendix I *Reproduction Doorways*

Beginning in the 1920s Connecticut River Valley doorways, especially those with scroll pediments, began to be reproduced with various degrees of skill. Some, milled-out at the lumber yard, are easily recognizable for what they are and can be found on twentieth-century houses as well as on those of the eighteenth century. Others, hand-crafted under the guidance of such knowledgeable antiquarians and architectural historians as J. Frederick Kelly, who designed the flat-top doorway for the Dr. Alexander King house in Suffield, may easily be confusing. Early scroll doorway reproductions are on the Samuel Pond house (Curtis Funeral Home), Branford, Connecticut; the Joseph Root house (Tavern), Montague, Massachusetts, designed for Ardelia R. Hall in 1932 by the Boston architect John E. Linnett and based on the MFA's doorway (56) from the Elihu White house, Hatfield (papers in possession of present owners Paul F. and Hannah Neville); the home of Mr. and Mrs. Carlyle Eubank on Route 57 in West Granville, Massachusetts, made by Rudolph Hendrick; the Will Liebler house (1981 owner) on Route 85 near Gilead, Connecticut; and the Joshua Stoddard house at 381 Hartford Avenue, Wethersfield. About 1930 the Northampton architect Karl S. Putnam built a brick house for Mr. and Mrs. Lucius D. Potter on Franklin Street in Greenfield, Massachusetts, for which he designed an excellent reproduction triangular pedimented doorway.

A reproduction segmental pediment on the Martin Sheldon house in East Granby, Connecticut, was apparently based on the John Thompson III house in Farmington (132). The doorway on the so-called Sidebottom house in Fairfield, Connecticut, is an early reproduction as is the flat-top in Eastford, Connecticut, made by a Mr. Black in the 1920s. The flat-top doorway on the Daniel Linley house (Evarts Tavern) in Northford, Connecticut, was made by the father of William V. Schanz (the 1981 owner), who came from Germany.

Steve Racz of Milford made convincing reproduction doorways in the 1940s and 1950s as did William E. Gass of South Deerfield, who was responsible for scroll doorways on the Reverend Jonathan Ashley house and on the Dwight Barnard house, both in Deerfield.

And doorways continue to be reproduced. In the 1970s doorways appeared on two houses in Hatfield, one on the Elisha Hubbard house (Tavern) and one on the Col. Oliver Partridge house where disturbed clapboards gave evidence of a former pediment. In recent times four newly made scroll doorways in Massachusetts have appeared, one in South Hadley, one in Sheffield, one in Wilbraham, and one in Westfield.

Caution is advised with regard to the identification of reproduction doorways, some constructed so long ago that present local historians are unable to recall the time they were not on the house. And recent owners of houses with early reproduction doorways are frequently unaware that the doorway is not of eighteenth-century construction.

Appendix II *Joiners.*

Of the many joiners who resided and worked in the Connecticut River Valley in the eighteenth century whose names are known from account books, land and probate records, as well as from local histories and genealogies, only the names of those who can be associated with specific work on a particular house or doorway or who are thought to have influenced joiners who worked on doorways are here listed. As previously noted in the Introduction, a number of joiners associated with eighteenth-century Connecticut River Valley doorways are also known to have been furniture makers. The dual role of these joiners is documented below.

BELDEN, Return (1721-1764) was the son of Josiah and Mabel (Wright) Belden of Rocky Hill (Wethersfield), Connecticut. He apprenticed as a joiner with William Manley of Wethersfield about 1735-1742. For the period from February to March 1740, Elisha Williams (1718-1784) charged Manley in his account book (WHS) for purchases made by "Belding y^r Apprentice," and on 12 August 1740 Williams noted that he owed Manley for "Cash p^d to return Belding 15/7." In February 1745 Williams arranged for Return Belding to make items of furniture for his third cousin, the Reverend Chester Williams of Hadley, who had married Sarah Porter on 23 August 1744. The account of Elisha Williams with Return Belden lists "1 Chest of Draws £ 16-0-0, 1 Tea Table 1-7-6, 1 phanned Dressing Table £ 5-0-0, Casing the above all for M^r W^{ms} hadley 7/6." When Return Belden died unmarried, an inventory of his estate (CSL) listed various wood-working tools and "forty two Schuchens [escutcheons] for Desk." His legal heirs were his brothers Solomon Belden and Josiah Belden, his sisters Mabel Griswold and Lydia Churchill, and his brothers-in-law Maj. Josiah Griswold and Capt. Charles Churchill. Return Belden may have worked on the scroll pedimented doorway on Capt. Charles Churchill's house in Newington (20) and on the triangular pedimented doorways for Maj. Josiah Griswold's house in Wethersfield (100).

CLARK, Isaac (d. 1762) was a resident of Windsor, Connecticut, at the time of his death. His inventory included numerous joiner's tools. He married Ruth _____, who in 1782 was the wife of _____ Higley. In 1739 and 1740 Clark was paid for work on the meeting house for the First Society in Hartford (First Society Records, CHS). In 1757 he was paid £ 2-9-03 for work on the house of Ebenezer Grant in South Windsor (29).

EASON, Ahimaz (b. 1739), son of Elijah and Sarah (Spencer) Eason, was probably born in East Hartford, Connecticut, and was the first cousin of James Eason and Oliver Eason, both joiners. In 1762 he sold a homelot in Suffield and purchased one in Westfield. The deeds gave his occupation as "Joyner." According to a Westfield deed of 1766, his wife was Mary. In 1767 Ahimaz Eason sold his homelot in Westfield and probably moved away at that time. He was listed in the 1790 census as a resident of Hudson, New York. Although no specific work of Ahimaz Eason can be documented, he is a strong candidate for one of the joiners who built the Daniel Fowler doorway in Westfield (63), a hypothesis supported by the fact that his name appears in the account books of Ebenezer Grant of South Windsor in the 1750s, indicating that he was familiar with Grant's doorway (29), which is so similar in decorative detail to the Fowler doorway. Ahimaz Eason may have also worked on houses and doorways in Sheffield (206) and in Northampton (120), Massachusetts, which have pedestals with miniature scroll doorways similar to those on the Grant house.

EASON, James (1728-1796), son of Joseph and Susannah (Burnham) Eason, was born in East Hartford, Connecticut, and was a first cousin of Oliver Eason and of Ahimaz Eason, both joiners. In 1751 his first wife Rachel Seymour died in West Hartford, and in 1753 he married Eunice Pomeroy of Northampton. In 1762 James Eason was living in Litchfield, where he probably worked on the Second Meeting House (12) completed that year. In 1763 he settled in Pittsfield and may have worked on the house of the Reverend Thomas Allen (59). In 1764 James Eason was the master-joiner in the construction of Christ Church, Great Barrington (Dow, p. 219, quoting *Boston News Letter, 19 July 1764*). In 1766 James Eason built three schoolhouses in Pittsfield (*Pittsfield History*, p. 136). An inventory of his estate taken 7 November 1797 listed "Sundry Joiner's Tools 1.50."

EASON, Oliver (1732-1761) was born in East Hartford, Connecticut, and died there probably unmarried. He was the son of Timothy and Prudence (Buckland) Eason and a first cousin of James Eason and of Ahimaz Eason. Included in Oliver Eason's inventory were numerous itemized joiner's tools and hardware for case furniture. In 1754 and 1755 he worked on the house of Samuel Colton (57) in Longmeadow and on 24 June 1754 he and John Steel, Jr., were credited in Colton's account book for "Work Don at a Dore." Eason worked about thirty-four days and Steel, twenty-eight. Only the elaborate scroll pedimented front doorway on Samuel Colton's house could have required this amount of labor. On 5 December 1754 Oliver Eason was credited in the account book of Elijah Williams of Deerfield for thirty days' work (see 48). He had gone straight to Deerfield from Longmeadow since he had made a purchase at Colton's store on 19 October 1754.

FABRIQUE, Bartimus (ca. 1750-1829), a joiner of Southbury, Connecticut,

and

FABRIQUE, David (ca. 1745-1798), a housewright of Newtown, Connecticut, were the sons of John Fabrique, a French Protestant who settled in Connecticut. The subjects of meticulous research by William L. Warren, who located the papers of the Fabrique brothers in the Historical Records Collection at the Sterling Library at Yale University, Bartimus and David Fabrique were active in Fairfield, New Haven, and Litchfield counties in Connecticut. According to Warren, they worked on the Second Meeting House in Southbury, finished about 1779 or 1780; on the Episcopal Church in Newtown; and on the Second Meeting House in Oxford, completed in 1795. A dwelling house in Southbury, about eight hundred feet south of the intersection of Routes 6 and 67 and owned in 1959 by Mr. and Mrs. Donald Moore, was probably built by Bartimus Fabrique about 1800 (*Woodbury Homes*, p. 202). Among the Fabrique papers is an architectural drawing labelled "Plan for Roxbury Meeting House." The design called for a scroll pedimented doorway, but the meeting house (26) built in Roxbury, Connecticut, in 1795 may not have followed the Fabrique plan. The first of Warren's publications on the Fabriques (Warren, *Oxford*) appeared in the June 1981 issue of the *Connecticut Antiquarian*. The same author has deposited a manuscript, "Descendants of John Fabrique (1696-1782) of France and Newtown, Connecticut," at The Connecticut Historical Society.

GRANT, Aaron (1724-1804) was born and died in South Windsor, Connecticut, the son of Samuel Grant and brother of the joiners Abiel Grant and Alexander Grant. In 1751 he married Mabel Eason, daughter of Samuel and Sarah Eason and first cousin of the joiners Ahimaz Eason, James Eason, and Oliver Eason. According to the account books of his uncle Ebenezer Grant of South Windsor, Aaron Grant was paid £ 47-19-03 for work on Grant's house (29) in 1757 and £ 30-11-2 for work done from 1757 to 1761 on the Third Meeting House in South Windsor (30). On 29 February 1764 Ebenezer Grant allowed Aaron Grant credit on a purchase in his shop "toward Case draws." In his will dated 1 January 1799 (CSL) Aaron Grant left his joiner's tools to his sons Aaron Grant and Epaphras Grant.

GRANT, Abiel (1729-1762) was born and died in South Windsor, Connecticut, the son of Samuel Grant and brother of the joiners Aaron Grant and Alexander Grant. According to the account books of his uncle Ebenezer Grant, Abiel Grant was paid £ 19-06-08 for work on his uncle's house (29) in 1757 and £ 68-16-2 for work on the Third Meeting House (30) from 1757 to 1761. An inventory of Abiel Grant's estate (CSL) listed materials for house construction and for furniture making such as window frames and sashes, white pine, shingles, cherry boards, glue, brads, and slitwork as well as numerous itemized joiner's tools.

GRANT, Alexander (ca. 1736-1801) was born in South Windsor, Connecticut, the son of Samuel Grant and brother of the joiners Aaron Grant and Abiel Grant. The account book of his uncle Ebenezer Grant shows that Alexander Grant was paid £ 62-12-2 for work done from 1757 to 1761 on the Third Meeting House in South Windsor (30). In 1764 Alexander Grant purchased a homelot in Westfield and may have worked there on the house and doorway of Daniel Fowler (63), which is similar in decorative detail to the doorway on his uncle's house in South Windsor (29). Although Alexander Grant did not work on the Ebenezer Grant doorway, two of his brothers did; and Alexander Grant was certainly familiar with it. He may also have worked on the Ashley house in Sheffield (207) and the Parsons house in Northampton (120), both again sharing decorative features found on the Grant doorway such as foliage carving and pedestals with miniature scroll pediments. Alexander Grant married two times. His first wife Thankful Lyman of Northampton, whom he married in 1768, died in 1770. His second wife Miriam Sexton of Enfield, Connecticut, widow of David Bliss, was the mother of his son Erastus Grant who became a furniture maker in Westfield (Bulkeley).

GRAY, Abiel (1715-1805) was born in Andover, Connecticut, the son of Robert and Miriam Gray. In 1744 and 1745, at a time when Ebenezer Grant's account book credits Gray with unspecified work, he was a resident of Tolland; but later he settled in Coventry. He was listed in the 1790 census as a resident of Hartford. In 1739 Abiel Gray was paid for work on the meeting house for the First Society in Hartford (First Society Records, CHS), and in 1757 he was credited in the accounts of Ebenezer Grant of South Windsor for joiner's work on his house (29) to the amount of £ 46-11-07.

KING, Parmenas (1713-1800) was a son of Thomas and Sarah (Mygatt) King of Hartford, Connecticut, and a brother of Zadock King (1725-1769), a joiner who settled in Deerfield. In 1735 he moved to Harwinton, Connecticut, as one of the first settlers (*Harwinton History*, p. 109). By 1741 King was living in Enfield. On 4 August 1741 a land transaction recorded in Hampshire County, Massachusetts, called him Parmenas King of Enfield, "Joyner." On 31 December 1741 he married Hannah Terry of Enfield. About 1764 he moved to Windsor where he remained until 1768 when he moved to Wilbraham, Massachusetts, where he was residing at the time of his death. He is buried in Wilbraham.

Although the work of Parmenas King cannot be documented to any specific doorway in the Connecticut River Valley, he was credited in the account books of Samuel Colton of Longmeadow with considerable joinery work on Colton's house (57). On 7 May 1754 Colton recorded, "Permenas King Came here to Work Late in the morning"; and on 15 July 1754 Colton noted, "Permenas King Enfield Came here to Work a munday after noune he Work^d 4½ Days." At the end of October and during November 1754, King worked for Elijah Williams of Deerfield (see 48) whose account book credited Parmenas King with thirty-seven days' work on 5 December. Like Oliver Eason, King had gone to Deerfield straight from Longmeadow as indicated by a purchase made at Colton's store on 22 October 1754.

On 22 April 1758 King was credited by Samuel Colton "By Work 3 Days With Y^r Boy"; and in 1767, as recorded by Colton, King worked on Longmeadow's second meeting house (113) that had been raised on 18 June 1767.

The most significant entry in Colton's accounts with regard to King appeared on 20 July 1754 when Colton recorded, "Permenas King Enfield Took a pies of Work to Dow for £ 50 New Hampshire money old ten, he is To Doe all the Work on the Est Side of the house & north End that blongs to out Side Work & paint the End & Side & Key & Set the glace." Apparently included in this agreement concerning the east (front) and north side of Samuel Colton's house was all joinery work with the exception of the scroll doorway constructed by Oliver Eason and John Steel, Jr. Parmenas King may thus be regarded as the maker of the triangular window pediments with elm tree devices on Colton's house, one of which survives in the collection of SPNEA. This positive identification suggests that King may have been responsible for other pediments of similar design on windows and doorways in the area (See Appendix IV, Similar Features).

MANLEY, William (d. 1787), a furniture maker of Wethersfield, Connecticut, was probably born in Charlestown, Massachusetts. When his son William Manley, Jr., was baptized in Wethersfield on 14 March 1731, the Reverend Stephen Mix noted that the father "belonged to Charlestown." According to Wethersfield records, four children were born there to William and Mary Manley: William 1731, Margaret 1732, George 1735, and Ebenezer 1737. On 19 December 1720 a William Manley married Mary Tolman, daughter of Thomas Tolman of Needham, Massachusetts, who was born 4 October 1697 (*NEHGR* 14:249). The reason for William Manley's move from Charlestown to Wethersfield during 1729-1731 may never be known, but the date of the move coincided with the death of the Charlestown joiner Nathaniel Frothingham in 1730 (Bjerkoe, p. 98) and suggests a possible association between the two.

In 1740 Elisha Williams (1718-1784) of Wethersfield charged his then un-married aunt Elizabeth Williams of Hatfield for cash he had paid to William Manley on her behalf for a chest. He noted in his account book (WHS), "Elizabeth Williams Hatf^d . . . July 17 [1740] to cash p^d Mr. Manly for Chest Draws 20-0-0." In 1740 Return Belden was apprenticed to William Manley. Manley may have also trained the joiner Samuel Partridge.

When William Manley wrote his will on 17 May 1787 (CSL), he described himself as William Manley of Windsor ". . . Being Greatly Advanced in Years & much Infirm as to Bodely Health But of Sound minde & memory. . . ." His legatees were his sons William and George, his daughters Mary, Margaret, and Sarah, and his grandsons Allyn, Russell, and William, sons of his son Ebenezer, deceased. An inventory taken 12 December 1787 listed "a heap of Pine bords . . . an old Shop . . . a heap of Chery bords Estimated at 1000 feet." His house was identified as being near the Simsbury line.

William Manley cannot presently be associated with any specific doorway, but as the master of Return Belden, the possible master of Samuel Partridge, and as a direct link between the wood-working traditions of eastern Massachusetts and the Connecticut River Valley, William Manley occupies a central position.

PARTRIDGE, Samuel (1730-1809), a joiner, a lieutenant in the French and In-dian War, and a tavern keeper in Hatfield was born in Hadley, Massachusetts, the son of Cotton and Margaret (Cook) Partridge. When he was three, his father died; in 1736 his mother married Samuel Gaylord of Hadley. A half-brother, Samuel Gaylord, Jr., born in 1742, also became a joiner.

Samuel Partridge may be proposed as the joiner of a number of doorways in Hadley and further afield, although documentation is sparse. Reasoning in-evitably begins with a tall clock, owned by descendants of Samuel Partridge, bearing the inscription "Lieut Samuel Partridge 1730-1809 'The old Leftenant.' " As indicated on the face of the clock, the works were assembled by Obadiah Frary of Southampton; the case was the work of Partridge who crowned the hood with a scroll pediment. At the termination of the scrolls are six-petal rosettes with centers consisting of three points lined vertically and flanked by vertical elipses. While no other clock case decorated with these par-ticular rosettes is known, identical rosettes appear on doorways. One doorway with these rosettes, that on the house of Elijah Williams in Deerfield (48), can safely be attributed to Partridge. On 4 September 1760 Williams recorded in his account book a debt to Samuel Partridge of £ 39-0-2 for "work on my house." This sum represents the largest amount that Williams paid to any joiner.

Rosettes of this design are also found in Wethersfield on the Simeon Belden house (41), but whether or not Samuel Partridge worked on the Belden house, it seems likely that he trained as a joiner in Wethersfield. According to the standard system of apprenticeship, Partridge would have begun to learn his trade about 1744-1745 at a time when the work of Wethersfield joiners was patronized in Hadley. On 14 July 1750 a twenty-year-old Samuel Partridge was in Wethersfield and was apparently then a resident although he had no close relatives there. Elisha Williams (1718-1784) recorded a purchase in his account book (WHS) listing not Samuel Partridge of Hadley but merely the entry "Samuel Partridge D^r 1750 July 14 To 3½ yds Check @ 14/6 2-10-9." There exists the strong possibility that about 1744 or 1745 Samuel Partridge journeyed to Wethersfield to train as a joiner, perhaps with William Manley or with Return Belden.

Figure 8 Tall clock by Obadiah Frary, Southampton, Massachusetts; case by Samuel Partridge. (Private collection)

By early 1753 Partridge, who would have recently completed his training, was employed by Joshua Warner of Hatfield for some unspecified joinery work. Seth Dwight of Hatfield recorded in his account book (FoL), "Joshua Warner D^r . . . February 1753 to 121 feet of Bords thick stuff Delivered Sam Partridge." In 1753 Partridge was living in Hadley when in a deed of 6 April he was called "Joyner." A week later on 14 April 1753 he purchased a half interest in the homelot of Seth Dwight across the river in Hatfield. On 18 January 1754 Samuel Partridge married Abigail, daughter of Seth Dwight. Having settled in Hatfield, Partridge had sold his homelot in Hadley on 5 January 1754.

In November 1754 Elijah Williams of Deerfield employed the Connecticut joiners Parmenas King and Oliver Eason to work on the old house built by the town for his father in 1707. Samuel Partridge was also in Deerfield and made frequent purchases at Elijah Williams's shop. Further, it is clear that Partridge was in the company of King and Eason when they visited Williams's shop together as indicated by adjacent entries. Partridge, however, was not credited with any work by Williams. Samuel Partridge, whose earlier training may well have been in furniture making, may have taken this opportunity to observe the techniques of the two house joiners.

On 2 July 1756 Elijah Williams recorded a debt to John Bull of Deerfield for "Bording Partridge & Printes 11 Days." On this occasion Partridge had travelled from Hatfield to Deerfield to work for Elijah Williams. The apprentice with him may have been Partridge's half-brother, Samuel Gaylord, Jr., about to turn fourteen. When Williams noted his debt of £ 39-0-2 to Partridge on 4 September 1760, it was for work on a new house.

If the scroll doorway on the Elijah Williams house can be attributed to Partridge on the basis of rosettes similar to those on Samuel Partridge's tall clock and on the large sum owed to him by Elijah Williams, it follows that Partridge's skill as a joiner was recognized outside his native Hadley and his adopted Hatfield. Had there been an equally competent joiner in Deerfield in the 1750s and 1760s, there would have been no need for Williams to send for Partridge and thus to increase his cost with boarding expenses. It also follows that other nearly identical doorways in the area, closely resembling the doorway on the Elijah Williams house, those with fluted pilasters, mushroom finials, and the six-petal rosettes, can also be attributed to Samuel Partridge.

Based on overall proportion and on similar secondary moldings as well as similar rusticated surrounds, other less restrained doorways decorated with foliage carving on pilaster caps, keystones, finial bases, and occasionally as a substitute for fluting also appear to be by the same hand.

During the 1760s students at Hatfield Academy frequented the tavern of the versatile Samuel Partridge on the west side of Hatfield's street (Judd diaries). But Partridge was still active as a joiner in 1774 when on 19 September he was again in Deerfield. His purpose was to supervise extensive renovations on an old house purchased by the Field family the previous year in anticipation of the coming marriage of Elihu Field (Ashley papers, Elihu Ashley [L. Blake] to Polly Williams, 17 May 1773). On 19 September 1774 Elihu Ashley wrote in his diary, ". . . then went to E. Fields house found Lieut Partridge. . . ." (This house still stands on the east side of the Deerfield street toward the north end of town. About 1816 the house was remodelled and enlarged by Ebenezer Hinsdale Williams to the point where it is difficult if not impossible to detect the hand of Partridge although eighteenth-century panelling does survive. Now the property of Historic Deerfield, Inc., the house is generally known as the Cowles house.)

Hatfield town records list the following death in 1809, ''April 4 Samuel Partridge Etatis 79 Chronical gout.'' Houses with doorways attributed to Samuel Partridge include examples located in Deerfield (46, 47, 48, 106, 186); Hadley (50, 194); Hatfield (52, 54, 55, 56); Stockbridge (61, 62); and Hinsdale, New Hampshire (129).

Figure 9   Detail of hood. Obadiah Frary/Samuel Partridge tall clock. (Private collection)

SALMON, Thomas (ca. 1693-1749), as the designer of Christ Church (31) in Stratford, Connecticut, was responsible for the earliest known scroll pedimented doorway of the Connecticut River Valley type, a doorway probably executed about 1744-1749. To Salmon are also attributed doorways in Stratford with heavy projecting pediments such as the curved front pediment and triangular back pediment on the David Judson house (33).

Of unknown parentage, Salmon emigrated from England to settle in Stratford at least by 1720 and perhaps earlier. His wife Sarah, daughter of William Jeans (Janes), gave birth to his first child, Robert Salmon, in Stratford in October 1720.

In the burying ground of the Episcopal Church in Stratford stands the now largely defaced gravestone of Thomas Salmon. Readable except for the bottom line as late as 1959, the epitaph states:

Here Lies the Body of
Mr Thomas Salmon who
was born in Chippenham in
England, & was a worthy
member of ye Church of
England here & ye ingenious
Architect of this Church
& Departed this Life Janr^y
20th 1749-50 in ye 57th year of
[his life.]

From this epitaph can be learned Salmon's birthplace, the approximate year of his birth, his church affiliation, and his major role in the building of Christ Church in Stratford, none of which might otherwise be known; although Salmon bequeathed land in Chippenham in Wiltshire to several of his children in his will, he did not state in that document that he was born there.

Efforts to discover a baptismal record for Thomas Salmon in Chippenham, and thus learn the identity of his parents, received the following response from W.C. Rathbone, the Wiltshire County Archivist, on 24 May 1966: "I have searched the baptismal register [for Chippenham] from 1690 to 1700, but can find no baptism of Thomas Salmon, nor of any person of that Surname." Mr. Rathbone also attempted to trace Salmon's land in Chippenham and in the same letter to AFM reported: "I have looked at the parish rate books for various years in the early 18th century, but cannot trace any property belonging to the family. Our indexes here do not refer to anyone of the name in connection with Chippenham."

Donald R. Friary discovered a William Salmon who was a carpenter in Potterne about fifteen miles southeast of Chippenham. On 26 March 1721 Richard Gale, son of John Gale, was apprenticed to William Salmon, carpenter of Potterne, and on 24 June 1723 Hugh Hillman was apprenticed to William Salmon, carpenter of Potterne (Dale). Friary speculated that Thomas Salmon may have been a son of William the carpenter who learned his trade from his father and whose apprenticeship was thus never officially recorded. However, in correspondence with AFM in 1966 the Reverend John T. Davis, vicar of the church at Potterne, who searched the parish register spanning the years from 1670 to 1790, found no Thomas Salmon but did find children of a William and Mary Salmon: Samuel born 1712, Elizabeth born 1714, Patience born 1716, and Joan born 1718. A William Salmon, probably the carpenter, died on 8 October 1727. A Mary Salmon, probably the carpenter's widow, married Hugh Wilkins on 1 January 1731. Perhaps William the carpenter was an older brother of Thomas Salmon.

The temptation to search for a relationship between Thomas Salmon of Chippenham, Wiltshire, and William Salmon, author of, among other architectural guides, *Palladio Londinensis*, is always there. However according to H.M. Colvin, *Biographical Dictionary of British Architects*, this William Salmon was a carpenter of Colchester in Essex, far to the east of Wiltshire. Further research in England is clearly indicated. To know the parents of Thomas Salmon would be interesting, but of equally great importance would be to uncover a relationship with William Salmon of Colchester and to learn where and with whom Thomas Salmon trained.

One matter that can be resolved satisfactorily is the conflict involving the year of Salmon's death. His gravestone states that he died on 20 January 1749/50. Probate records (CSL) contradict the 1750 date. Among these records are a will dated 7 January 1748/49, a testimony that the will was presented at court on 3 March 1748/49, and an inventory dated 4 April 1749. Clearly Salmon died in 1749, probably on 20 January; and the year given on his gravestone is inaccurate. Salmon's wife followed him closely to the grave, dying on 15 March 1750, creating the possibility that both gravestones were erected at some time subsequent to the calendar change in 1752 and that the error on Thomas Salmon's stone can be attributed to confusion related to the new style of dating.

Of the many unanswered questions concerning Thomas Salmon, perhaps the most unsettling is the matter of his influence on Connecticut River Valley architecture in general and on doorways in particular. Was his scroll pedimented doorway on Christ Church in Stratford a major influence?

STEEL, John, Jr. (b. ca. 1729) was the son of John Steel, a cordwainer who resided in Westfield, Massachusetts, in 1728 and who married Abigail Brooks of Longmeadow, then a part of Springfield, on 7 March 1728. On 31 October 1751 John Steel, Jr., married Eunice Crowfoot in Longmeadow. In 1750 John Steel, Sr., had sold his homelot in Longmeadow to his son John Steel, Jr., "Joyner"; in 1752 John Steel, Jr., sold that homelot to Richard Woolworth, cordwainer. On 24 June 1754 Samuel Colton of Longmeadow credited "Olever Eson & John Steel 2 [Jr.] Work Don at a Dore. . . ." Eason worked about thirty-four days and Steel, twenty-eight. Only the elaborate scroll pedimented front doorway on Samuel Colton's house (57) could have required this amount of labor. John Steel, Jr., continued to work for Samuel Colton and to purchase commodities from Colton's store until 11 April 1757, the date of the last entry for Steel and the last known record concerning him.

VINING, Josiah (1733-1794) was born in Windsor, Connecticut, the son of Josiah and Mary (Gleason) Vining who were both residents of Enfield, Connecticut, at the time of their marriage in 1727. Josiah Vining was paid £ 16-7-14 for joinery work on the house of Ebenezer Grant of South Windsor (29). At the time of his death in 1794, Josiah Vining was a resident of Danbury, Connecticut; and the name of his wife was Mary.

WOODRUFF, Judah (1722-1799) was born in Farmington, Connecticut, the son of Joseph and Elizabeth (Curtis) Woodruff. In 1753 he married Eunice, daughter of William and Ruth (Lee) Judd of Farmington. A captain in the French and Indian War, Judah Woodruff has long been known to architectural historians. In 1872 Noah Porter (1811-1892), then president of Yale, delivered an address at a celebration of the hundredth anniversary of the Third Meeting House (149) in which he acknowledged Judah Woodruff as the architect and master builder (*Historical Discourse,* in Kelly, *Meeting Houses,* 1:162). Porter further related that Judah Woodruff built ten houses "including his own" in Farmington before the Revolution and "four or five" after the war was over. When questioned about the reliability of these statements, Mabel Spencer Hurlburt, the Farmington historian, explained in a 3 November 1959 letter to AFM that Capt. Judah Woodruff grew up with Noah Porter's grandfather whose son, the Reverend Noah Porter, was minister of the church in Farmington from 1806 until his death in 1866 and would have known Judah Woodruff in his childhood.

In 1766 and 1767 Judah Woodruff was credited with considerable joinery work on the house of Fisher Gay of Farmington (146) and also for items of furniture — a trundle bed, a clock case, and a cradle (Gay account books).

In addition to the Farmington meeting house (149) and Fisher Gay's house (146), both with flat-top doorways, the five other houses in Farmington with doorways of the Connecticut River Valley style are all considered to be the work of Judah Woodruff (19, 132, 145, 147, 148).

Appendix III *Author's Glossary of Improvised Architectural Terms*

Certain innovative features found on doorways of the Connecticut River Valley style have no descriptive names in the vocabulary of classical architecture. The following terms have been devised to describe these unique forms.

BRICKWORK RUSTICATION. Simulated masonry, carved to resemble brick courses, occasionally used to decorate pedestals.

COMPRESSED ENTABLATURE. Narrow and poorly defined architrave, pulvinated frieze, and cornice.

DOUBLE ROSETTE. A small cluster of petals outlined by larger petals giving the effect of a double set of petals.

DOUBLED OUTLINE. A device adding depth or dimension to a doorway as pilasters, keystones, pedestals, and other elements were set off by recessive and matching molded outlines, called WINGWAYS by Edward Hoppus (*The Gentleman's and Builder's Repository, or Architecture Displayed*, London, 2d ed., 1738).

DUCK-BILL KEYSTONE. A keystone pinched at the top, rounding outward then curving inward, with a horizontal termination.

ELM TREE DEVICE. In triangular pediments, window and doorway, a slim applied vertical piece reaching from the center of the base to the apex where in the soffit of the triangle a projection of the bed molding spreads outward to resemble the silhouette of an elongated fan or elm tree.

FAT MOLDINGS. An exaggeration of the base molding of the pilaster.

RAISED CORNERS. A projection forward of the bed molding and cornice within the corner angles of a triangular pediment, largely found on window pediments.

RUFFLED. Alternating astragals with fillets and fluting, tapering downward; found occasionally on pilaster caps and keystones, similar to those illustrated by Batty Langley. (See in particular: *The Builder's Director, or Bench-Mate*, London, undated ed., and *The Workman's Golden Rule*, London, 1756).

S PANELS. Panels divided by a rail having the contour of a broken S, echoing the profile of a scroll pediment.

THUMB-PRINT DECORATION. Horizontal rows of small carved indentations used occasionally to decorate a keystone or pilaster cap.

X PANELS. Panels in the form of a cross, illustrated by William Salmon (*Palladio Londinensis*, 5th ed., London, 1755, pl. 23) with the comment, "The Manner of Pannelling the lower Part of this Door is exceeding strong and ornamental."

Appendix IV *Similar Features*

As Connecticut River Valley joiners visited neighboring towns and as they changed their place of residence, certain features on doorways and interior panelling became widespread and common in use. The duck-bill keystone, the petalled rosette, and X panels are among these. Other forms not so common, Ionic volutes, flame finials, and foliage decorated pilaster caps, probably carved to imitate Corinthian capitals, were illustrated in builders' guides, thus permitting individual joiners in widely separated areas to arrive at similar but individual interpretations. However, some doorways share unusual features that, if not the work of a single joiner, at least sprang from a common source. Triangular pediments with elm tree devices, probably the work of the joiner Parmenas King, fall into this category. The following lists identify doorways and other joinery whose features are so nearly identical as to suggest either a common hand or a common source.

1. Pilasters with brickwork pedestals.
    Doorways: 202, 206, 215. *Panelling:* 57 (presently at Smithsonian Institution, formerly identified with the Reuben Bliss house, Springfield, Massachusetts). *Other:* Corner cupboard presently at Winterthur Museum believed to have a Farmington origin.
2. Pedestals with miniature scroll in base.
    Doorways: 29, 63, 207. *Panelling:* 120 (interior). *Other:* Desk and bookcase with foliage carving topped by miniature scrolls at Henry Ford Museum.
3. Pilasters with fans at base of fluting.
    Doorways: 137, 168, 197. *Panelling:* interiors of the Abraham Burbank, John Granger, and Alexander King houses, all Suffield, Connecticut.
4. Pilasters with vine (tulip and grape) carving.
    Doorways: 56, 62, 134. *Panelling:* interior of the Reverend Samuel Hopkins house formerly Hadley, Massachusetts, present location now thought to be Greenwich, Connecticut. *Other:* Corner cupboard from the Elisha Hubbard house, Hatfield, Massachusetts, now reportedly removed to Maine.
5. Pilasters with foliage caps.
    Doorways: 29, 207. *Panelling:* 120.
6. Pilasters with foliage caps, topped by petals.
    Doorways: 46, 50, 61, 195.
7. Pilasters with two vertical lozenge-shaped tablets.
    Doorways: 137, 167, 168, 197.
8. Pilasters with multi-petalled rosettes in combination with ornate keystones.
    Doorways: 37, 57, 60, 189. *Panelling:* interior of the Reverend Samuel Hopkins house, Hadley, Massachusetts.
9. Rosettes at termination of scrolls with four double-leaf petals.
    Doorways: 46, 50, 52, 56, 61, 62.
10. Rosettes with six-pointed stars.
    Doorways: 20, 29.
11. X panels with an arch panel at top.
    Doors: 57, and the Col. Elisha Buell house, Marlborough, Connecticut. *Panelling:* room at the MMA traditionally believed to be from Newington, Connecticut (said by Elmer D. Keith to have come from a house other than Newington, possibly 57).

12. Triangular pediments with elm tree device.
   Doorways: 113, 118 (side), 120, 124. *Windows:* 37, 57, 60, 113, 118, 120.

[202]   Brickwork pedestal. Detail of doorway from an unknown house in Montgomery, Massachusetts, installed on the Reverend Phineas Fiske house in Haddam, Connecticut.

[29] Pedestals with miniature scroll. Detail of the doorway of the Ebenezer Grant house, South Windsor, Connecticut.

Figure 10 Foliage carving topped by miniature scrolls. Detail, desk and bookcase, Connecticut River Valley, eighteenth century. Henry Ford Museum and Greenfield Village.

[137] Pilaster with fan. Detail of doorway of the Luke Thrall house, East Granby, Massachusetts.

[134] Pilaster with vine carving. Detail from the doorway of the John Dickinson house, Hatfield, Massachusetts.

[29] Pilaster with foliage cap. Detail from the doorway of the Ebenezer Grant house, South Windsor, Connecticut.

[50] Pilaster with foliage cap topped by petals. Detail from the doorway of the Samuel Porter house, Hadley, Massachusetts.

[137] Pilaster cap with tablets. Detail from the doorway of the house of Luke Thrall, East Granby, Massachusetts.

[189] Pilaster with multi-petalled rosette. Detail from the doorway of the Abraham Burbank, Jr., house, Feeding Hills, Massachusetts.

[29] Rosettes with six-pointed stars at termination of scroll. Detail of the doorway on the Ebenezer Grant house, South Windsor, Connecticut.

[57]   Elm tree device. Window pediment from the Samuel Colton house, Longmeadow, Massachusetts. S.P.N.E.A.

Abbreviations Used in the Text

AFM   Amelia F. Miller
AHS   Ashfield Historical Society, Ashfield, Massachusetts
AL   Acton Library, Saybrook, Connecticut
CHS   Connecticut Historical Society, Hartford, Connecticut
CSL   Connecticut State Library, Hartford, Connecticut
FaL   Farmington Library, Farmington, Connecticut
FoL   Forbes Library, Northampton, Massachusetts
GHS   Glastonbury Historical Society, Glastonbury, Connecticut
HD   Historic Deerfield, Inc., Deerfield, Massachusetts
HNFL   Henry N. Flynt Library of Historic Deerfield, Inc.
LC   Library of Congress, Washington, D.C.
LHS   Litchfield Historical Society, Litchfield, Connecticut
LmHS   Longmeadow Historical Society, Longmeadow, Massachusetts
MFA   Museum of Fine Arts, Boston, Massachusetts
MMA   Metropolitan Museum of Art, New York, New York
NEHGR   *New England Historical and Genealogical Register*
NHCHS   New Haven Colony Historical Society, New Haven, Connecticut
NYHS   New York Historical Society, New York, New York
OTNE   *Old-Time New England*
PVMA   Pocumtuck Valley Memorial Association, Deerfield, Massachusetts
RL   Russell Library, Middletown, Connecticut
SM   Skinner Museum, South Hadley, Massachusetts
SPG   Society for the Propagation of the Gospel in Foreign Parts
SPL   City Library, Springfield, Massachusetts
SPNEA   Society for the Preservation of New England Antiquities, Boston, Massachusetts
SLY   Sterling Library, Yale University, New Haven, Connecticut
SWL   South Windsor Library, South Windsor, Connecticut
WA   Wadsworth Atheneum, Hartford, Connecticut
WeA   Westfield Athenaeum, Westfield, Massachusetts
WHS   Wethersfield Historical Society, Wethersfield, Connecticut
WiHS   Windsor Historical Society, Windsor, Connecticut

List of References Cited

Public Records

Land and probate records were kept differently in Connecticut and Massachusetts in the eighteenth century and continue to be so to the present time.

In Connecticut, land records were kept by individual towns and may be found today bound in volumes in town offices or city halls. Connecticut land records are also available on microfilm at the Connecticut State Library in Hartford where are also deposited most probate records up to 1850 (also on microfilm) and individual parcels or packets of loose probate papers all compiled early in this century. At the State Library are also church records and extensive files of vital records gathered from town, church, Bible, cemetery, and newspaper sources.

In Massachusetts both land and probate records have historically been kept by county authorities. Until the mid-eighteenth century Hampshire County occupied all the territory west of Worcester County to the New York state line. In 1761 Berkshire County was set off on the west. Franklin County, bordering on Vermont, was set off on the north in 1811 and Hampden County, bordering on Connecticut, was set off on the south in 1812. This left Hampshire County in the center of the state with jurisdiction on both sides of the Connecticut River. Land records before these divisions are located in Springfield; probate records, in Northampton. Vital records to 1850 have been published for many Massachusetts towns under a state-sponsored program. Original vital records are kept by each town and may be found at town or city halls at the office of the town clerk.

Unpublished Sources

Ashley diary.	Ashley, Elihu. Diary 1773-1775, PVMA library.
Ashley papers.	Ashley family papers, PVMA library.
Barnard, Joseph account books.	Barnard, Joseph. Account books. PVMA library.
Barnard, Salah account books.	Barnard, Salah. Account books. PVMA library.
Barber drawings.	Barber, John Warner. Drawings ca. 1830, CHS.
Christ Church Records.	Records of Christ Church, Stratford, Connecticut.
Colonial Dames.	Records of Early American Houses, compiled by the Colonial Dames, CSL.
Colton account books.	Colton, Samuel. Account books, LMHS.
Dwight Barnard House.	St. George, Robert Blair. "The Dwight-Barnard House: A Study in American Adaptation." Historic Deerfield, Inc., Summer Fellowship Program, 1975, HNFL.
Dwight, Josiah account book.	Dwight, Josiah. Account book. SPL.
Dwight, Josiah day book.	Dwight, Josiah. Day book. SPL.

Dwight, Seth account book.
Dwight, Seth. Account book. FoL. (Catalogued as Dwight, _____ account book, Hatfield, 1728-1761; internal evidence indicates that these were the accounts of Seth Dwight.)

Farmington Catalogue.
Hurlburt, Mabel Spencer. Farmington, Catalogue of Old Houses, compiled 1950s.

Friary.
Friary, Donald Richard. "The Architecture of the Anglican Church in the Northern American Colonies: A Study of Religious, Social, and Cultural Expression." Ph.D. diss., University of Pennsylvania, 1971. HNFL.

Gay account books.
Gay, Fisher. Account books. CHS.

Gay memoranda.
Gay, Rev. Ebenezer. Memoranda. Copy CHS.

Grant account books.
Grant, Ebenezer. Account books. Privately owned, formerly on loan to CHS.

Judd diaries.
Judd, Jonathan, Jr. Diary, 2 February 1768 to 29 July 1803. 4 vols. FoL.

Judd ms.
Judd, Sylvester, 1784-1860, comp. The Judd Manuscript. 64 vols., n.d. (uncatalogued, unclassified). FoL.

Pease diary.
Pease, Joseph. Diary. Copy CHS.

Punderson account book.
Punderson, Rev. Ebenezer. Account book. CHS.

Trumbull account books.
Trumbull, Jonathan. Account books. CHS.

Whitefield, SPNEA.
Whitefield, Edwin. Sketchbooks, ca. 1882. SPNEA.

Williams, Elijah account books.
Williams, Elijah. Account books. PVMA library.

Williams, Elisha account book.
Williams, Elisha. Account book. WHS.

Williams, Ephraim and Elijah account book.
Williams, Ephraim, and Williams, Elijah. Account book. PVMA library.

Published Works

Abbott.
Abbott, Katharine M. *Old Paths and Legends of the New England Border.* New York, 1907.

Ashley Genealogy.
Trowbridge, Francis Bacon. *The Ashley Genealogy: A History of the Descendants of Robert Ashley of Springfield, Massachusetts.* New Haven, 1896.

Ashley pamphlet.
Chase, Arthur C. *The Ashleys: A Pioneer Berkshire Family.* Trustees of the Reservations, n.d.

Barber, *Connecticut.*
Barber, John Warner. *Connecticut Historical Collections.* 2d ed., New Haven [1837].

Barber, *New Haven.*
Barber, John Warner. *History and Antiquities of New Haven, Conn.* New Haven, 1856.

Bennington Sketches.
Merrill, John, and Merrill, Caroline R. *Sketches of Historic Bennington.* Cambridge, 1907.

Beers Atlas, *New Haven County.*
Atlas of New Haven County, Connecticut. New York: F.W. Beers and Co., 1868.

Beers Atlas, *Hampshire County.*
Atlas of Hampshire County, Massachusetts. New York: F.W. Beers and Co., 1873.

Bjerkoe.
Bjerkoe, Ethel Hall. *The Cabinetmakers of America.* New York, 1957.

Bulkeley.

Chamberlain, *Doorways.*

Cheshire County Homes.

Chicopee Street.

Colonial Homes.

Connecticut History.
Connecticut Valley History.

Cornwall Records.

Crawford.

Crofut.

Dale.

Dow.

East Hartford History.

Farmington Homes.

Franklin County Map.

Great Barrington History.
Greenfield History.

Hadley History.

Hampshire Gazette.
Hartford County Biographies.
Hartford County History.
Hartford History.

Harwinton History.

Hatfield History.

Historical Discourse.

Kelly, *Houses.*

Kelly, *Meetinghouses.*

Kensington Church.

Bulkeley, Houghton. "George Belden and Erastus Grant, Cabinetmakers." CHS *Bulletin* 27, no. 3 (July 1962):65-73.
Chamberlain, Samuel. *New England Doorways.* New York, 1937.
Smith, Marjorie Whalen. *Historic Homes of Cheshire County New Hampshire.* Brattleboro, Vt., 1968.
Palmer, Clara Skeele. *Annals of Chicopee Street.* Chicopee, Mass., 1898.
Love, William DeLoss. *Homes of Colonial Times.* Hartford, 1914.
Sandford, Elias B. *A History of Connecticut.* Hartford, 1887.
History of the Connecticut Valley in Massachusetts. 2 vols. Philadelphia, 1879.
Gold, S. Theodore. *Historical Records of the Town of Cornwall.* Hartford, 1877.
Crawford, Mary Caroline. *Little Pilgrimages Among Old New England Inns.* Boston, 1907.
Crofut, Florence S. Marcy. *Guide to the History and the Historic Sites of Connecticut.* 2 vols. New Haven, 1937.
Dale, Christabel. *Wiltshire Apprentices and Their Masters, 1710-1760.* Devizes, Wilts., England: Wiltshire Archaeological and Natural History Society, Records Branch, 1961.
Dow, George Francis. *The Arts and Crafts in New England, 1704-1775.* Topsfield, Mass., 1927.
Goodwin, Joseph O. *East Hartford: Its History and Traditions.* Hartford, 1879.
Farmington, Connecticut. The Village of Beautiful Homes. Hartford, 1906 (unpaged).
Map of Franklin County, Massachusetts. New York: Smith and Ingham, 1858.
Taylor, Charles J. *History of Great Barrington, Massachusetts.* Great Barrington, 1882.
Thompson, Francis M. *History of Greenfield, Massachusetts.* 2 vols. Greenfield, 1904.
Judd, Sylvester. *History of Hadley . . . Massachusetts.* Northampton, 1863.
Hampshire Gazette. Northampton, Massachusetts.
Commemorative Biographical Record of Hartford County Connecticut. Chicago, 1901.
Trumbull, James Hammond. *The Memorial History of Hartford County, Connecticut, 1633-1884.* Boston, 1886.
Love, William DeLoss. *The Colonial History of Hartford.* Hartford, 1914.
Chipman, R. Manning. *The History of Harwinton, Connecticut.* Hartford, 1860.
Wells, Daniel White, and Wells, Reuben Field. *A History of Hatfield, Massachusetts.* Springfield, 1910.
Porter, Noah. *An Historical Discourse Delivered at the Congregation of the One Hundredth Anniversary of the Erection of the Congregational Church in Farmington, Conn., October 16, 1872.* Hartford, 1873.
Kelly, John Frederick. *The Early Domestic Architecture of Connecticut.* New Haven, 1924.
Kelly, John Frederick. *Early Connecticut Meetinghouses.* 2 vols. New York, 1948.
Two Hundredth Anniversary Kensington Congregational Church. Kensington, 1914.

Little.   Little, Nina Fletcher. *American Decorative Wall Painting, 1700-1850*. Sturbridge, Mass., 1952.

Living With Antiques.   Winchester, Alice, ed. *Living With Antiques*. New York, 1941.

Longmeadow Ses-   Longmeadow's [Massachusetts] Sesquicentennial Official
   quicentennial.   Souvenir. Longmeadow, 1933 (unpaged).

Mansfield History.   *Mansfield: A Passing Sketch of the Village*. Willimantic, Conn., 1880 (unpaged).

Mission House.   Eaton, Walter Prichard. *The Mission House, Stockbridge, Massachusetts* (undated and unpaged pamphlet available at the house), n.p.

Morris History.   Weik, Laura S. *One Hundred Years' History of Morris, Connecticut, 1859-1959*. Morris, Conn., 1959.

Newbury History.   Wells, Frederick P. *History of Newbury, Vermont*. St. Johnsbury, Vt., 1902.

New Haven Green.   Blake, Henry T. *History and Antiquities of New Haven Green from 1638-1862*. New Haven, 1898.

Northfield History.   Temple, J.H., and Sheldon, George. *History of the Town of Northfield, Massachusetts*. Albany, 1875.

Northampton Book.   *The Northampton Book*. Northampton, 1954.
*Northampton   Clark, Rev. Solomon. *Antiquities, Historicals and Graduates
   Graduates*.   of Northampton*. Northampton, 1882.
Northampton Homes.   Kneeland, Harriet J. *Some Old Northampton Homes*. Northampton, 1909.

Norwich History.   Caulkins, Francis Manwaring. *History of Norwich, Connecticut*. Hartford, 1874.

Norwich Homes.   O'Keefe, Marian K., and Doroshevich, Catherine Smith. *Norwich Historic Homes and Families*. Stonington, Conn., 1967.

Norwich Houses.   Perkins, Mary Elizabeth. *Old Houses of the Ancient Town of Norwich*. Norwich, 1895.

*Old-Time Meeting   Wight, Charles Albert. *Some Old-Time Meeting Houses of
   Houses*.   the Connecticut Valley*. Chicopee Falls, Mass., 1911.
Orcutt.   Orcutt, Rev. Samuel. *A History of the Old Town of Stratford and the City of Bridgeport, Connecticut*. 2 pts. New Haven, 1886.

Parsons House.   *The Parsons House of the Northampton Historical Society*. Northampton Historical Society, 1972.

*Picturesque Hamp-   *Picturesque Hampden, Part II — West*. Northampton, 1891.
   den*.
Pittsfield History.   Smith, J.E.A. *The History of Pittsfield, Massachusetts, 1734-1800*. Boston, 1869.

Plymouth History.   Atwater, Francis, comp. *History of the Town of Plymouth, Connecticut*. Meriden, 1895.

*Reclaiming the Old   Hooper, Charles E. *Reclaiming the Old House*. New York,
   House*.   1913.
Savage.   Savage, James. *A Genealogical Record of the First Settlers of New England*. 4 vols. Boston, 1860-1862.

Seymour Family.   Jacobus, Donald Lines. *The History of the Seymour Family*. New Haven, 1939.

Sheldon.   Sheldon, George. *A History of Deerfield, Massachusetts*. 2 vols. Deerfield, 1895, 1896.

South Hadley.   Eastman, Sophie E. *In Old South Hadley*. Chicago, 1912.
Springfield Sketches.   Chapin, Charles Wells. *Sketches of the Old Inhabitants . . . of Old Springfield. . . .* Springfield, Mass., 1893.

Springfield Union.   *The Springfield Sunday Union and Republican*. Springfield, Mass.

Stanton House.   *The Stanton House*. Stonington, Conn., n.d.

Stockbridge History. Jones, Electa F. *Stockbridge, Past and Present.* Springfield, Mass., 1854.

Suffield Anniversary. *Suffield Quarter Millennial, Celebration of the Two Hundredth and Fiftieth Anniversary of the Settlement of Suffield, Connecticut.* Suffield, 1921.

Summerson. Summerson, John. *Architecture in Britain 1530-1830.* Baltimore, Maryland, 1954.

Sunderland History. Smith, John Montague. *History of the Town of Sunderland, Massachusetts.* Greenfield, Mass., 1899.

Trent. Trent, Robert F. *Hearts and Crowns: Folk Chairs of the Connecticut Coast, 1720-1840.* New Haven, Conn., 1977.

Trowbridge. Trowbridge, Bertha Chadwick, ed. *Old Houses of Connecticut.* New Haven, 1923.

Trumbull. Trumbull, John. *Autobiography, Reminiscences and Letters of John Trumbull, from 1756 to 1841.* New Haven, 1841.

Warren, *Fitch.* Warren, William L. *Isaac Fitch of Lebanon, Connecticut, Master Joiner, 1734-1791.* Hartford, 1978.

Warren, *Oxford.* Warren, William L. "The Oxford Meeting House." *Connecticut Antiquarian* 33, no. 1 (June 1981):4-8.

Warren, *Talcott.* Warren, William L. "The Talcott Settle." *Connecticut Antiquarian* 29, no. 1 (June 1977):23-33.

Waterbury History. Anderson, Joseph. *The Town and City of Waterbury, Connecticut.* . . . 3 vols. New Haven, 1896.

Westfield History. Lockwood, John Hoyt. *Westfield and Its Historic Influences, 1669-1919.* Westfield, Mass., 1922.

Westfield Souvenir. *Souvenir of the Fair — Given by the Woman's Auxiliary.* 2 vols. Westfield, Mass., 1900.

Westhampton History. *Memorial of the Reunion of the Natives of Westhampton, Mass., September 5, 1866.* Waltham, Mass., 1866.

Wethersfield Doorways. *Homes and Doorways of Old Wethersfield.* Wethersfield Women's Association, 1927 (unpaged).

Wethersfield History. Stiles, Henry R. *The History of Ancient Wethersfield, Connecticut.* 2 vols. New York, 1904.

Whitefield, *Connecticut.* Whitefield, Edwin. *Homes of Our Forefathers . . . Rhode Island and Connecticut.* Boston, 1882.

Whitefield, *Vermont.* Whitefield, Edwin. *The Homes of Our Forefathers . . . Maine, New Hampshire and Vermont.* Reading, Mass., 1886.

White Pine. *The White Pine Series of Architectural Monographs.* White Pine Bureau, St. Paul, Minnesota, 1915-1939.

Wilcoxson. Wilcoxson, William Howard. *History of Stratford, Connecticut, 1639-1939.* Stratford, 1939.

Windsor History, 1859. Stiles, Henry R. *The History of Ancient Windsor, Connecticut.* New York, 1859.

Windsor History, 1892. Stiles, Henry R. *The History and Genealogies of Ancient Windsor, Connecticut.* Rev. ed. 2 vols. Hartford, 1892.

Windsor New History. Howard, Daniel. *A New History of Old Windsor, Connecticut.* Windsor Locks, Conn., 1935.

Woodbury History. Cothren, William. *History of Ancient Woodbury, Connecticut.* 3 vols. Waterbury, Conn., 1871.

Woodbury Homes. *Homes of Old Woodbury.* Old Woodbury Historical Society, Waterbury, Conn., 1959.

Index

(Numerals refer to page numbers; boldface numerals indicate the reference is part of a checklist heading.)

Photo and Illustration Credits

(Numerals refer to entry numbers; d signifies detail.)

PVMA, photo by Frances S. and Mary E. Allen: *Cover*, 48, 106.

SPNEA: *Figure 1*, *Figure 2*, 37d, 41d, 57, 57d, 147, 180.

CHS: 20, 20d, 25, 25d, 29, 37, 101.

Stratford Historical Society: 33.

Courtesy, The Metropolitan Museum of Art; gift of the estate of Ogden Codman, 1951: *Frontispiece*, 5.

Courtesy, The Metropolitan Museum of Art; Rogers Fund: 63.

Historic American Buildings Survey: 50, 134.

Deerfield Academy: 48d.

Photo by AFM: 29d, 29d, 55d, 62.

Collection of AFM, photo by Frances S. and Mary E. Allen: 56.

Collection of AFM: 60, 115, 119, 168, 191.

Collection of AFM, photo by Richard Merrill: *Figure 8*, *Figure 9*.

Collection of AFM, photo from Delphina Clark: 2.

Courtesy, Museum of Fine Arts, Boston: 56d, 57d.

NHCHS: 18.

Southington News: 27.

Courtesy, Christ Church Stratford, Conn.: 31, 31.

Forbes Library, photo by Lewis H. Kingsley: 52d.

Forbes Library, photo by A.W. and C.E. Howes: 55.

Forbes Library: 118.

Windsor Historical Society: 102.

Courtesy, Henry Ford Museum: *Figure 10*.

Photo by Daniel and Jessie Lie Farber: 29d, 46d, 50d, 56d, 134d, 137d, 163, 189d, 202d.

Photo by Peter Benes: 12d.

Drawn by Peter Benes: *Figures 3 through 6* (maps).

A Note About the Author

Amelia F. Miller began her career as an architectural historian while an undergraduate at Smith College, when she did research in Deerfield, Massachusetts, for Mr. and Mrs. Henry N. Flynt, founders of the Heritage Foundation, now Historic Deerfield, Inc. Since that time, as a resident of Deerfield, she has authored *The Reverend Jonathan Ashley House*, published by the Heritage Foundation in 1962, has written forewords for both the 1972 (with Donald R. Friary) and the 1982 reprints of George Sheldon's *A History of Deerfield*, co-authored *Turley Family Records* (1981), and has written for various publications including *The Magazine Antiques*, *Old-Time New England*, and *The Connecticut Historical Society Bulletin*. She is a member of the Pocumtuck Valley Memorial Association, the Connecticut Historical Society, and the Society for the Preservation of New England Antiquities.